The Leadership Imperative

About GatenbySanderson

GatenbySanderson is leading the way in developing people and organisations. We offer a joined-up approach to improving capacity and performance within the public sector. Our core services include:

Finding the best talent
Our experienced recruitment consultants, some of the most successful in the business, will attract, source, select and recruit the best talent for your organisation. We have an impressive track record in securing executive appointments and assisting our client organisations in achieving their diversity targets.

Transitional leadership
Our innovative approach to interim management. Our highly professional and experienced temporary placements successfully assist clients in creating capacity and achieving goals in the short to medium term.

Developing people
A comprehensive range of bespoke development services for both management teams and individuals. These include our very successful futurepotential programme, through which we help to develop the leaders of tomorrow.

Developing organisations
Tailored programmes of support designed to meet the performance improvement and development needs of your organisation.

About Demos

Who we are
Demos is the think tank for everyday democracy. We believe everyone should be able to make personal choices in their daily lives that contribute to the common good. Our aim is to put this democratic idea into practice by working with organisations in ways that make them more effective and legitimate.

What we work on
We focus on six areas: public services; science and technology; cities and public space; people and communities; arts and culture; and global security.

Who we work with
Our partners include policy-makers, companies, public service providers and social entrepreneurs. Demos is not linked to any party but we work with politicians across political divides. Our international network – which extends across Eastern Europe, Scandinavia, Australia, Brazil, India and China – provides a global perspective and enables us to work across borders.

How we work
Demos knows the importance of learning from experience. We test and improve our ideas in practice by working with people who can make change happen. Our collaborative approach means that our partners share in the creation and ownership of new ideas.

What we offer
We analyse social and political change, which we connect to innovation and learning in organisations. We help our partners show thought leadership and respond to emerging policy challenges.

How we communicate
As an independent voice, we can create debates that lead to real change. We use the media, public events, workshops and publications to communicate our ideas. All our books can be downloaded free from the Demos website.

www.demos.co.uk

First published in 2005
© Demos
Some rights reserved – see copyright licence for details

ISBN 1 84180 154 2
Copy edited by Julie Pickard
Typeset and produced by utimestwo, Northamptonshire
Printed in the United Kingdom

For further information and
subscription details please contact:

Demos
Magdalen House
136 Tooley Street
London SE1 2TU

telephone: 0845 458 5949
email: hello@demos.co.uk
web: www.demos.co.uk

The Leadership Imperative

Reforming children's services
from the ground up

Hannah Lownsbrough
Duncan O'Leary

DEM⊙S

DEM⊙S

Contents

Acknowledgements

First and foremost, we would like to thank Simon Jones, Carole Gayle, Caron Macmillan and all at GatenbySanderson for their support for the project. Paul Skidmore's help and advice throughout the research has been extremely valuable, as has Tom Bentley's guidance on writing the final pamphlet. Beyond Demos, particular thanks to Ian Birnbaum, Rob Tabb and Mark Simmonds for their advice during the writing process.

Other colleagues at Demos also looked at the draft and offered their perspective – especial thanks to Sophia Parker, John Craig, Simon Parker and Sarah Gillinson. Julia Huber, Sam Hinton-Smith and Abi Hewitt were crucial to producing and communicating ideas in the final report. Helen Trivers, Kate Mieske and Josephine Werdich all made important contributions during their internships with Demos.

Finally, we would like to thank all the people who agreed to be interviewed for the project, as well as those who took the time to attend the development seminar.

Hannah Lownsbrough
Duncan O'Leary
December 2005

1. Introduction

Every inquiry has brought forward proposals for change and improvement to the child protection system. There have been reforms. Things have got better for many. But the fact that a child like Victoria Climbié can still suffer almost unimaginable cruelty to the point of eventually losing her young life shows that things are still very far from right. More can and must be done.
Prime Ministerial foreword, *Every Child Matters*[1]

The *Every Child Matters* reform agenda represents one of the most significant changes to local children's services in living memory. Seeded by ongoing frustration at the failure to level the playing field for the country's most vulnerable children, the development of the policy took place in the shadow of several high profile preventable child deaths, most notably Victoria Climbié's. As a result, the new legislation and the accompanying guidelines call for a major overhaul in almost every aspect of children's services provision.

The reforms are radical not just because of their goal of prevention, but also because of the aspiration to combine guaranteed minimum standards of care and accountability with a universal service framework, focused on outcomes for *all* children. This demands that professionals from different disciplines work together in new ways, that separate organisations such as schools, children's centres and voluntary organisations collaborate to meet shared objectives. Local authorities need to promote integration and accountability while simultaneously encouraging greater flexibility in service provision.

Most estimates suggest that the full implications of the new structures, roles and responsibilities will take at least a decade to become embedded in the working practices of the professionals who will be implementing them on the ground. Equally, for local government officials administering the policy, the coming changes will imply a major upheaval in their approach. The schools white paper, published in October 2005, with its emphasis on creating a much more diverse range of providers within the education system, represents the next stage in a series of deep changes to the whole framework of schooling and children's services.[2]

Education reform is always politically controversial. But, in one sense, the changes brought by *Every Child Matters* have been exceptional. The professionals responsible for delivering the new services have embraced their overarching aims. The five goals identified through consultation (see box 1) reflect the long-held views of workers from a spread of backgrounds, who share a belief that a continuous improvement in outcomes from schools, social services and paediatric healthcare will be possible only if they work together far more closely, removing the discontinuities in support that impede children's progress.

Box 1 The five outcomes for children
1. Be healthy
2. Stay safe
3. Enjoy and achieve
4. Make a positive contribution
5. Achieve economic well-being

The danger for *Every Child Matters*, then, lies not in an outright rejection from the people being asked to deliver it, but in the day-to-day difficulties of making it work on the ground. Entrenched patterns of professional behaviour lead to scepticism and distrust of the capabilities of professionals from other backgrounds. The temptation to return to familiar habits in the face of major uncertainty can be powerful.

In other words, changes to structure and policy that are intended to generate a transformation of working practices can too easily be neutralised by prevailing professional identities and behavioural norms. When this happens, there is a risk that the outward appearance of integration is an illusion. In reality, the cracks between services can be just as deep – and, in some senses, more of a threat because there is now even more to conceal them. This, in turn, will have a direct impact on children themselves, who may experience a poorer quality service than when the dislocations between different elements of provision were at least openly acknowledged.

To guarantee that this is not what happens, we need to look beyond the conventional levers of control offered by making national policy and adjusting structures of authority, accountability and control. It is only by changing the culture of children's services that lasting success will be achieved. Through the operating context that it creates for children's services, central government can do much to encourage positive cultural change. But the solutions also rest on other foundations, and vary across each different local authority setting.

Rather than focusing exclusively on national policy we need to concentrate on the possibilities that will emerge at a local level. There are various springboards for creating that change: the views of children and their families, commitment among frontline staff, and the political impetus that comes from elected local councillors, to name just a few. But among these options the one with the greatest leverage – that which has the potential to create the greatest impact – is the leadership of local organisations with a stake in providing children's services, including Children's Trusts themselves.

By setting the tone for the working relationships between professionals – the extent to which children and families have their voices amplified within services – and mediating the relationship with political representatives, leadership can effectively create the context in which culture change is a valued goal for everyone.

Framing a shared leadership agenda, however, is particularly challenging, precisely because it must operate across many different organisations and between different levels of government, and because it must engage different professionals, families and communities within its reach.

This challenge resonates across the range of public service reform: as patterns of service provision become more diverse, with more providers and more flexible means of delivery, achieving coherence and shared objectives becomes far more important, just as some of the traditional, centralised methods of control and coordination become redundant. Using leadership to help overcome professional and organisational barriers, while promoting service innovation which generates better outcomes for children, is vital.

In *The Leadership Imperative* we explore the key opportunities for building such an agenda for leadership in children's services.

The Leadership Imperative

In the following chapter we identify the three key challenges facing children's services, we examine the policy response to them and we also explore some of their underlying causes. In chapter 3 we discuss the temptation for leaders to attempt to 'fix' problems on our behalf, and we make the case for a much deeper cultural shift in children's services. In chapters 4 to 7 we discuss some of the ways in which leaders can work towards changing the culture of organisations. Finally, in chapters 8 and 9 we outline the role that national policy has to play in supporting the changes that government aspires to, and in contributing to the cultural change that will ultimately underpin them.

2. Key challenges

Confronting the three key challenges

Children's services face three main obstacles to achieving the outcomes for which they are now accountable, and to sustained improvement in service quality. They are:

O *Separation*: services that fall under the 'children's services' umbrella are still disconnected from one another
O *Standardisation*: the offer made to children in schools, social services and health provision tends to be 'one size fits all'
O *Risk aversion*: the approach of professionals at all levels of children's services is often profoundly risk averse – more centred on preventing bad things happening than enabling good things to come about.

Separation

It is well known that very few people who are accessing public services are addressing only one issue at the time when they engage and that issues arising in different facets of their lives affect the likely success of policies targeted at only one area. The success of interventions such as Sure Start and Youth Offending Teams testify to the fact that multi-agency services are very often better placed to meet people's needs, particularly those of the most vulnerable. The policy on children's services stemmed from the findings of the Laming Report about the potential risk linked with having disconnected services, with gaps between provision.[3]

But the story from local authorities is that services are still dislocated from one another. In part, this is because of some of the logistical difficulties with bringing together previously separate organisations. But it is also to do with the culture clash between professionals from different arenas. Historical tensions arising from fights for limited resources and different strategic approaches can also make it hard for shared working practices to gain purchase with frontline staff.

Training for teachers, social workers, doctors and nurses starts with very different assumptions about the best ways to do their work. That can cause problems with trust when they work together.

Standardisation

To achieve the sort of transformational change that children's services could represent will work only if users of services are placed at their centre. Social work has long advocated the use of individually tailored solutions for people in difficult circumstances.[4] Equally, education practice is increasingly favouring a 'personalised' approach, with learners encouraged to be the architects of their own experiences during school.[5] For other elements of public services, the rhetorical commitment to personalisation has not moved into the realities of services delivery, partly because of misperceptions about the different resource requirements needed to deliver tailored services.

By bringing together a range of professionals, children's services should create new opportunities for delivering tailored solutions to individual service users. An increasingly diverse range of options for users will improve individuals' experiences only if they can be understood by the people accessing them. Central to this is creating a system which can personalise the offer that it makes to children and young people; otherwise, the choices between different possibilities run the risk of being more complex, without being more effective.

But attempts to personalise services are still confronting serious challenges, as professionals grapple with new delivery arrangements, which will increasingly be commissioned from local authorities, and service managers seek to harmonise practices across a local area without letting the quality of services deteriorate.

Developing a personalised approach has been challenging for professionals operating within their traditional fields. But as the understanding of what tailored services can mean has grown, it demands that people reach beyond those boundaries to deliver services that are integrated with one another. This combination of circumstances – a renewed commitment to personalising services, while also learning about a series of new working relationships – has made creating a sustainable model of personalisation one of the key tests faced by children's services.

Risk aversion

Public services designed to deliver services to children are always particularly challenged by the issue of risk. The possibility that a child could be harmed rather than helped by health workers, or the seriousness of their position overlooked by social services, is of major concern to practitioners and policy-makers. In addition, the strict chains of command that exist within schools, hospitals and local authority departments can create a culture where it is easy to pass blame from level to level.

In *The Risk Management of Everything*, Mike Power explains that we are increasingly operating in a climate where the focus on minimising risk is becoming paramount.[6] Although that may diminish identifiable dangers, it undermines the capacity of organisations to deal with unexpected and unpredictable risks, which can't be managed by creating protocols to reduce their impact. These risks are best tackled through equipping professionals with good judgement that they are empowered to use when it is needed.

This creates a culture in which people's first priority can often be to minimise risk, sometimes at the expense of developing new solutions to existing problems. For children's services to improve on existing modes of delivery, it is vital that people at all levels of local authorities are given the chance to identify new ways of working. Central to this is creating a setting in which people are able to discover and embrace new ideas.

The policy response

The challenges facing children's services are not new: the new approach represents the culmination of years of policy-making targeted at addressing these issues. The Children Act of 2004, which followed the *Every Child Matters* green paper, created a raft of new structures, roles and responsibilities, each measure designed to bring services together around the needs of young people. A summary of the Children Act, and subsequent legislation, is laid out in box 2.

Box 2 Summary of the Children Act 2004

New structures

O   provision for the creation of Children's Trusts in local areas, allowing for joint commissioning and delivery of children's services

O   provision for pooled budgets at the local level, to support this commissioning role.

New roles

O   a new children's commissioner for England to raise awareness of the interests of children and to report annually to parliament

O   the creation of a director of children's services in every local authority, bringing together (as a minimum) responsibility for education and social services

O   the creation of a lead member responsible for children's services on every elected ouncil

O   the creation of a new lead professional role in each case, to coordinate the delivery of children's services.

New responsibilities

O   a duty on local authorities to promote cooperation between the agencies involved in children's services

O   a requirement that local authorities set up local safeguarding boards

O   a requirement that local authorities establish a children and young people's plan outlining how children's services will be delivered in their local area, replacing current statutory planning duties

O   the requirement for an integrated inspection framework for children's services

O   the establishment of a joint area review, to assess the standard of all services delivered in a local area

O   an annual performance assessment, to assess the standard of services delivered in education and social services

O   a specific duty on local authorities to promote the educational achievement of looked-after children

O   an alteration to the inspection framework for schools to include formal responsibility for children's well-being.

A striking feature of the response from central government has been the high level of support that it has generated from practitioners themselves. Reactions to the consultation on the green paper were usually positive, as were the views of many of the professionals that we met during our research.

But the practicalities of change are testing people's resolve. A year on from the Children Act – and a few years in to some local programmes of change that pre-dated it – professionals are being asked to confront the daily realities of implementation, as well as the high-minded ideals that preceded it.

Understanding the causes

This transition from theory into practice is where the real challenge lies. Despite the genuine commitment to a new way of working, structural fixes can be part of the answer only because the three key challenges described above have their roots in deeply ingrained patterns of behaviour, which have developed over long periods of time. Therefore, while the authorities' transition from deliverers of local services to commissioners of them has captured the attention of the media, there are issues that go far deeper:

○ People habitually work in silos, both mental as well as institutional, developing a small group of professionals with whom they interact regularly and rarely moving outside their specialist area.
○ There is an ingrained expectation that professionals will know best in very many situations, making it difficult for users' voices to have a meaningful impact.
○ Children's services are constantly working in an environment where the stakes are extremely high and 'witch hunts' are not uncommon when things go wrong. As a result, there can be a disincentive for innovation, meaning workers are more likely to spend time ensuring their back is covered should anything difficult occur than to propose alternative ways of working.

Working in silos

The tendency of workers to create 'cliques' around particular areas of practice is unsurprising and, in some senses, reflects an important part of professional practice. Expertise and specialisation have developed over many years for a very good reason: they create professional norms and offer a network of support for decision-making in particular settings.

Equally, professional identities are strong within the public sector, reflecting the keen sense of vocation with which many workers enter their roles, meaning that people are perhaps less likely to look beyond their immediate professional boundaries to get advice or a fresh perspective.

In this sense, there is a place for creative conflict within public service delivery – not many of us would want prosecutors and judges to form multi-agency teams, because they serve different functions. Analysis of a child's particular needs by several different people can work to ensure that every angle of his or her particular position has been considered by someone who is expert within that sector. But if the conversations between professionals do not rest on a foundation of trust and understanding, then they risk lapsing into a competition between professionals, rather than a constructive debate about what the user needs to thrive.

For children's services, working across these divides will be essential if integration is to become a reality. At the moment, integration happens primarily as part of purposely designed initiatives, intended to bring workers together around particularly taxing issues that benefit from a coordinated response. Extended schools, for instance, have been established mostly in areas experiencing higher than average levels of deprivation. They aim to address educational underachievement within the local community through creating open institutions which deal with the wider issues that act as a barrier to learning, such as family breakdown and poor mental and physical health.[7] The challenge for children's services is to draw out the lessons from these isolated initiatives and establish them as overarching principles of supporting children.

This really will only be possible if we manage to address these issues together . . . leaders have to be able to deal with more of the picture.

Who knows best?

For services to become more personalised to the needs of individual users, professionals need to be prepared to engage with users' and carers' own accounts of their requirements. But this is difficult to achieve in a culture where the assumption that professionals know best has been ingrained since the original creation of the welfare state. In addition, professionals are still receiving conflicting signals from government about the strategies that they should use for developing and delivering services. As one health professional put it:

> *Trying to walk the line between user-led services and evidence-based practice is extremely difficult.*

Most pertinently, there are particular issues in relation to user-led services when the users of those services are children and young people and are therefore still developing. Two key dilemmas emerge. First, how do we judge the degree to which children are able to make decisions about their service provision, without overloading them with responsibility too early in their development? Second, in the case of vulnerable children who may be experiencing threatening situations, what level of choice about how their case is managed is appropriate?

There are also very different attitudes to user-led approaches within the different elements of children's services. While the professional and working cultures of social work have consistently emphasised finding solutions that are tailored, as far as possible, to individual needs, the scientific basis of much healthcare testifies to certain treatments being objectively 'better' for people than other approaches that the patient might request. So professionals are sometimes placed in a position where a good clinical decision could be the very opposite of the request made by a patient. Equally, in education, classroom numbers and limited access to technology mean that teachers have traditionally worked hard to find compromise strategies that take a negotiated line between the different needs, interests and learning styles of their students.[8]

These problems become more acute when the user in question is a child who, depending on their age and stage of development, may be struggling to make all of their own choices. Our capacity to make long-term judgements develops as we mature from child to adult and so children will often need additional support in making decisions about routes through different sorts of provision.[9] In other cases, a user's assessment of their own needs may differ from their carers' assessment. For example, the process of caring for a sick or disabled child means that a parent or carer is more cautious about the choices for a child than they are for themselves.

But despite these conflicts, involving users in the design of their services still has significant benefits, particularly for children and young people from challenging circumstances. The Who Cares? Trust, which advocates for children in care and facilitates children being involved in developing their own care planning, argues that it is essential for looked-after children to be heard in this way.[10] Likewise, improving certain health outcomes is impossible if the patient is not fully involved in finding solutions that will work for him or her personally. Managing conditions such as diabetes or prolonged mental health issues necessitate supportive behaviour from the patient and his or her family. For children's services to be as effective as possible, they must engage with drawing users and their families into the process of personalising services to meet their needs.

How do you create a culture where people naturally come together and prioritise the child?

High stakes

Risk is an inherent part of growth and development within any organisation.[11] For children's services, however, it presents a particularly challenging issue. Part of the impetus for the change in legislation came from some of the worst sorts of failure of risk management – the deaths of children that should have been (and in some cases, were) under local authority supervision.

In part, this issue demands that we address the 'myth of control' when it comes to child deaths. The ultimate goal of social services, and most services aimed at children, is to prevent terrible things from happening to them, and to ensure that they are given the chance to grow into happy, healthy and independent adults. When this does not happen, however, it is not an indication that the professionals working on that child's case did not have these priorities.

Although it is right that this aim continues to act as a focus for professionals, preventing child deaths should not become the overpowering focus for children's services for two main reasons. First, focusing on the worst-case scenarios at the expense of other areas reflects a misconception that every child death will be preventable: in a small number of cases, they will be virtually impossible to avoid. Second, generating protocols around a tiny percentage of very extreme cases will not engender better services for the vast majority of children accessing them. A universal service – which is what *Every Child Matters* prescribes – must give proper weight to children with moderate levels of need.

> *Judging the best level of intervention for a child with moderate needs – enough to support, and not so much that they feel swamped, or too many resources get used – can be really hard.*

Managing risk has always been a key focus for local authority social workers, as for those working in healthcare. The nature of the interventions that social services make within families has meant that, for many years, the extent to which a child is 'at risk' has been the justification for their involvement in particular cases. But with high-profile cases of school-based staff committing offences against children and children being killed or injured on school trips, risk has become an increasingly central concern for education professionals as well.

It is not only being responsible for children's well-being that creates risk aversion among professionals, however. The response to accidents or negligence when it does occur has increasingly taken the form of a 'witch hunt', tracing lines of responsibility down to individual workers who had made poor decisions, as well as focusing on systemic failings that would lead up to a more senior level of accountability.[12] For example, a tribunal found that Lisa Arthurworrey, the social worker fired by Haringey Council after Victoria Climbié's death, should have the ban on her working with children overturned, because it had been a disproportionate response.

> *Dealing with failures has often become focused on deciding blame.*

Although this is in keeping with trends elsewhere in the public sector – the decline in the convention of ministerial responsibility being one of the starkest examples in the last 20 years of government – it has serious implications for the enduring climate in which professionals are then asked to operate. Combined with the reports that emerge in the press – demonising social workers and describing court cases where teachers are tried and convicted for failing to protect their students – and the advice from unions that increasingly urges caution on their members – workers are very often in a position where even small risks can seem to be the start of a descent into professional disaster.[13]

All this anxiety about risk not only distracts from the conversation about the 'enabling', as well as the 'preventing', role of professionals, but also creates a major disincentive for innovation. Trying new things, or learning from past experiences, in an environment where failure is feared – no matter how serious it is – can be almost impossible.

Out of the comfort zone

These underlying causes conspire to create a series of comfort zones that professionals can easily be drawn back in to. Despite the genuine support for the values of *Every Child Matters*, professionals are faced with the constant challenge of not reverting to the safety of their organisational boundaries, their professional authority, or the risk management of everything. Life inside these traditional boundaries can be far less complex and threatening, and years of working in a particular fashion are not easily shed, however sincere our intentions.

In this tendency lies both the leadership imperative – the rationale for leadership itself – and the central task for leaders in all areas of children's services. Leadership is not simply a case of determining an overall strategy, but of ensuring that genuinely held professional aspirations are reflected in everyday working practices.

The temptation is to regard this as a question of better management, but it is more than this. In the next chapter we make the case that if lasting change is to take root, leaders must not expect to drive through large-scale reform simply by pulling on the traditional levers of 'implementation'. We argue that only through working towards genuine cultural shifts can leaders ensure that the high ideals of *Every Child Matters* are realised in practice.

3. Searching for solutions

When faced with a problem our instinctive reaction is to find someone to fix it. If something goes wrong in our house we hire an electrician or a plumber; if our car breaks down we call a mechanic; and if we feel unwell we visit a doctor. Similarly, in our organisations we appoint leaders.

In many cases, this represents an efficient way of solving problems – quite rightly we turn to expertise when we know it is available. In our organisations as complex as those involved in children's services, however, what Ronald Heifetz has described as the 'flight to authority'[14] can create dangerous levels of expectations of leaders.

Although the 'cult of the CEO', which was so prominent during the economic boom of the 1990s, is beginning to fade, our assumptions about how and where problems can be solved often still betray themselves. In the corporate world enormous salaries – and severance packages – persist, while in government, the identification of social problems invariably leads to the creation of 'tsars', or 'task forces', charged with finding solutions to issues as complex as crime, drug abuse and anti-social behaviour. Appointing a leader reassures people not just that something is being done, but also that someone is in place to do it.

In this respect, children's services offer no exception. The enormous challenges laid out by Lord Laming in his enquiry[15] have led to the creation of three new leadership positions in children's services. The Children Act of 2004 legislates for the creation of:

O a minister for children
O a lead member for children's services on every local
   council
O a director of children's services in every local authority.

Each of these roles has been widely welcomed, and each undoubtedly has an important part to play in helping to reshape children's services around the needs of every young person. However, the creation of every new leadership position brings with it a risk: of propping up an unsustainable model of leadership, in which leaders are repeatedly set up to fail. Just as we expect a mechanic or an electrician to solve problems on our behalf, we often require of our leaders that they find technocratic solutions to problems as complex and deeply ingrained as those discussed in the last chapter. Invariably those solutions do not exist. And despite the repeated failure of leaders to 'deliver' in this way, we rarely question our understanding of leadership itself. Instead we prefer to project our disappointment onto the individuals in charge of an organisation or system at any given time.[16]

Faced with such inflated expectations – which many leaders are themselves complicit in sustaining – those in authority often find themselves grasping for 'levers of change'. Problems can arise, however, when this imperative to deliver change focuses attention on the parts of a problem that appear fixable, rather than the issues that really lie at the heart of it. The danger is that the highly visible elements of organisational life, which appear on a leader's radar, receive the greatest attention, rather than those that really matter.

Frequently, it is organisational structures that meet these criteria of being both visible and easy to change. As leaders of children's services seek to overcome the problem of fragmented services, then, it will be easy to be drawn in by the comforting belief that some well-reasoned restructuring will bring about the required changes in their organisation(s).

As history attests, however, the record of restructuring is patchy at best. While some amalgamations have genuinely led to greater coherence and efficiency,[17] examples abound of restructuring in government that has failed to achieve the desired effect – only to be succeeded by a further round of restructuring.

The structural 'solution'

Similarly, in services organisations restructuring has often done more harm than good. As Ed Mayo commented in a recent publication from the National Consumer Council, 'The experience of the NHS since 1974 shows how incessant efforts to change the organisational structures and cultures can lead to constant churn, initiative fatigue and not a little cynicism on the part of those who work in and use the service.'[18] Box 3 outlines some examples of structural 'solutions' undertaken by government.

Box 3 Structural 'solutions' in government

O   In 1997 the government took the decision to merge three departments, creating the Department for Transport, Local Government and the Regions – only for this 'super department' to be subdivided again in 2001. After just four years, responsibilities were divided between the Office of the Deputy Prime Minister and the newly (re)created Department for Transport.

O   In 2000, at the height of the dotcom boom, the government launched its own e-university, heralding it as an organisation capable of giving UK higher education the capacity to compete globally with the major virtual and corporate universities. In 2003 the university was closed down, with estimated losses to the taxpayer of £50 million.

So why has restructuring failed to produce the desired results, and what does this mean for the prospects of Children's Trusts as vehicles for re-casting children's services as holistic and preventative solutions?

The key reason why restructuring has had such little impact in many – although not all – instances is that people can be incredibly resistant to change when it goes against the grain of organisational cultures. This does not mean that people are unable to adapt to change, but rather implies quite the opposite. As changes are made to the environment in which people work, they are often highly skilled in adapting to their new surroundings – and going back to working in exactly the same way as they did before.

This tells us something about the type of problem that leaders in children's services face. With sufficient knowledge it is possible to re-wire a computer to work in an entirely different way, but re-wiring an organisation (or, worse, a number of organisations) is not such a straightforward process. Changing people's job titles, or amalgamating departments, does not necessarily alter their perceptions of their own roles, or change their everyday working practices. As Tom Bentley has noted, the challenges facing the civil service – and the tools available to it – are in constant churn, but it remains resilient enough to maintain a recognisable identity and a consistent way of working over considerable periods of time.[19]

The budgetary 'solution'

In a similar vein, the Children Act allows for the establishment of pooled budgets between different organisations involved in the delivery of children's services. In the same way as restructuring offers a tempting 'fix' for leaders, pooled budgets also represent another potential cul-de-sac for leaders searching desperately for tangible changes directly within their reach.

Although the Children's Trust pathfinders have been positive about the potential for pooled budgets to help avoid duplication of services,[20] it will be important for leaders (and policy-makers) to resist the temptation of seeing shared budgetary arrangements as an end in themselves. The government's Improvement and Development Agency (IDeA) has warned that the process of establishing pooled budgets can be time consuming and difficult,[21] echoing advice from the Education Select Committee that 'pooling budgets often poses a range of challenges that can be extremely time consuming to resolve.

Partners need to be very clear about the added value of budget pooling, and their individual and joint commitment to the work before taking this route.'[22]

In this sense, the key point for leaders will be to ensure that budgets are aligned as much as they are *actually pooled*, in the search for coherence in children's services. Just as secondary schools have been able to weave together vast numbers of funding streams over the last five years – and continue to pursue their pre-existing priorities – pooled budgets offer no guarantee that that they will bring services together *per se*.

The accountability 'solution'

This continuing search for 'levers' of change, which will somehow allow leaders to rise to the challenge and 'fix' organisational problems, often leads us to accountability frameworks. Through establishing what gets measured, and by which criteria, audit and inspection actively shape the context in which they operate. In this regard, inspection offers a tool for leadership in both central and local government to set the agenda in children's services, as the recent changes to the inspection framework for schools demonstrate.[23]

As Mike Power and others have argued, however, the extensive use of inspection frameworks to close loopholes or widen responsibilities necessarily involves a drift towards centralisation, and a model of leadership based largely on compliance.[24] While, undoubtedly, such an approach has its place in a leader's repertoire, it rarely addresses the underlying problems of organisational culture and individual learning.

In this sense, the commitment generated to a new way of working is what Chris Argyris described as 'external commitment' – a willingness to follow the rules – rather than 'internal commitment' or a personal commitment to a new way of working.[25] Argyris argues that while external commitment has its benefits, it represents an essentially limited strategy. He suggests that it often leads only to 'gaming' of the rules, with only creative compliance taking place. While schools may have officially acquired a new set of

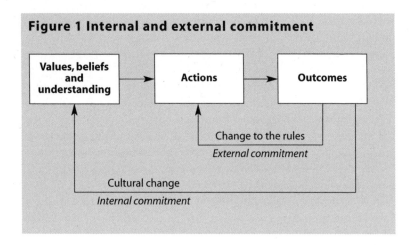

Figure 1 Internal and external commitment

responsibilities, then, the genuine test of changes in outcomes will be whether they embrace their new role, or simply devise the best way to be 'Ofsted-ed' every three years. In practice, this will have to depend on more than changes to legislation, and will require the kinds of cultural shift also necessary in other areas of children's services.

Figure 1 represents Argyris's argument.

Cultural change

This focus on bringing about cultural change is particularly pertinent in children's services, where the challenge for leaders is not just to alter one professional culture, but to align many different sets of professional values. For years teachers have understood their role through concepts such as 'learning', while social services have concerned themselves with 'well-being', and the police have worked to encourage and enforce 'respect for the law'. Furthermore, children's services increasingly involve a range of different providers, from the voluntary sector to private sector providers, with each of them bringing differing experiences, values and professional cultures with them.

Marrying these deeply held professional values in such a way that different organisations can work in a truly coherent fashion will require leaders capable of understanding not just *what* changes need to take place in their local areas, but also *how* this might happen in practice. As one police officer told us, 'the thing I hope I can help us all do is understand each other . . . then we can think about what joint interventions we can make'.[26]

Henry Mintzberg famously argued that there is no such thing as a gap between strategy and implementation, just strategies that don't take implementation into account,[27] and this points towards some core competencies for leaders of children's services, particularly in a system defined more by interdependence than by traditional forms of managerial power. While intellect, or the ability to see through a problem, will be important, emotional intelligence – the ability to take into account how different professionals view their own roles, and bring them together around shared objectives – will be at least as important.

Further, while there is clearly widespread and genuine support for the principles underpinning the *Every Child Matters* legislation, old habits die hard. The problems posed by fragmented services are not new,[28] and professionals can all too easily fall back into the comfort zone of their own professional silos, and their natural position of authority over children and young people. Both of these tendencies point towards mediocrity, rather than excellence, through undermining the principles of a more coherent and personalised set of services.

In order for leaders to generate the kind of change that both government and professionals are determined to bring about, therefore, leaders of children's services must begin to escape the temptation of the technocratic fix. Unquestionably, structural change, pooled resources and new accountability frameworks have their roles to play but, as we argue in the following chapter, leaders must be more ambitious – and more adept – than this. Changes to people's mental models, and shifts in organisational cultures, will hold the key to creating genuine and lasting change.

Making it work

Conversations with leaders in a range of positions with local authorities have revealed key themes in their approach to making cultural change happen within their organisations. First, there is a set of ideas relating to the inception of the new services, developing the right expectations and ground rules for moving forward. Second, all the leaders we spoke to had devised strategies for dealing with some of the negative consequences of bringing in change. Third, all of the leaders had a considered approach to the question of risk. And, fourth, they had found different strategies for building capacity for the next generation of leaders, and creating opportunities for people to grow within their roles.

4. Good foundations

The message of the system leaders we spoke to during the course of our research was clear: to get the changes right, it was crucial to get off on the right foot. They highlight two key principles:

O It is essential to create clear frameworks at the start of implementation.
O Structures can be used to send clear signals about the direction that change should move in.

Setting your stall out: creating clear frameworks at the beginning

Leaders in children's services emphasised the importance of having a clear outline at the start of a project. It provides a legitimate opportunity for everyone to feed in to the process of shaping the services before anything is concrete.

In one authority that we visited, the leaders also found this initial process can provide an opportunity to 'set the tone' in terms of user involvement – if children and young people can be involved at this earlier stage, then it helps to put their perspective at the heart of designing the services.

Children and young people have set the priorities for our services. And not only bigger kids, but little children as well, right down to toddlers.

By law, authorities are required to consult young people when putting together their Children and Young People's Plan (CYPP), but finding innovative ways of involving young people – and playing their voices into debates beyond children's services – can send a powerful message. Leaders can literally lead the way in putting children at the centre of services, while drawing young people into wider decision-making processes at their local level can also give practical expression to some of the government's aspirations around citizenship.

In Rotherham, for example, children have been positioned squarely at the centre of the planning process, with even toddlers brought into consultation exercises intended to communicate their views to councillors and officials. Likewise, the children's mayors in Lewisham – who are given a substantial budget to be spent on their priorities – have a genuine impact on the way services are delivered.

Clear plans early on also created clear boundaries for discussion and debate for the future. One director explained that, for her, consistency had been key to earning people's confidence; if there is a sense that changes are being made behind the scenes and targets are being moved without their knowledge, people will quickly lose faith in the changes they are being asked to deliver.

If you're not prepared for all of this, then you're going to be on the back foot.

But earning support for a wider process does not amount to having to make every decision by committee.[29] Leaders have to be prepared to make a decision – to have the 'casting vote' around issues about which there is dissent. The leaders we spoke to were able to make progress without seeking consensus from all their workers and users, having earned their trust through the process of seeking their views and taking them seriously.

Leaders have to be able to [make decisions] about more of the picture as a whole.

Furthermore, several leaders highlighted the importance of establishing shared frameworks early on, as a way of ensuring that the inevitable disagreements between professionals remain constructive rather than adversarial (see box 4). Lord Laming was clear in his report[30] about the importance of maintaining professional expertise during the process of integration, and this sentiment was universally supported among the people we spoke to during our research. Crucially, however, they argued that an agreed endpoint, or set of outcomes, is crucial in ensuring that debate between professionals can, in some sense, remain disciplined.[31]

What I want is a crunchy salad with lots of different flavours, not a mushy soup!

Box 4 Case study: Momentum and trust doesn't equal consensus
On Monday 19 September 2005, over 100 people gathered together in a room in the London Borough of Bexley to plan for the future of children's services in the area. With 38 different organisations – ranging from statutory services to a local premiership football club – represented on the day, the group was asked a single question:'What can we do better over the next three years to improve the life chances of young people?'
The day was never supposed to be easy. It brought together a range of people from different professional backgrounds and asked them to find practical solutions to problems in a way that 'consultation' processes rarely do. And the day began with a challenge from Deborah Absalom, the director of Children's Services:

O   to acknowledge that children and young people live in a world that brings pressures that many of us have not experienced
O   to begin, at least, with questions rather than answers

O   to use the local knowledge in the room to find the right
     solutions for the young people in Bexley

What followed was an Open Space event. In three sessions, groups
formed around the issues they judged to be important. If you felt
you could contribute to a group discussion you joined it. If not, you
simply left and joined a different one. Youth workers discussed
common issues with headteachers, Connexions advisers and
police. Some groups discussed emotional health and the well-
being of children; others tackled how to bring about seamless
services for young parents. By the end of the day, 60 separate
issues had been raised, recommendations had been developed,
and then prioritised by the whole group.

No one person attended anywhere close to all the discussions,
but it didn't matter. Not all the recommendations will find their
way into Bexley's Children and Young People's Plan – and those
that do won't match everyone's priorities. However, what the
session offered was a chance to bring together such a range of
professionals, to bring them out of their comfort zones, and to ask
them to contribute in a practical way.

There was no magical consensus at the end of the day, but what
it created, in addition to a wealth of practical steps to take forward,
was a sense of momentum and trust in the changes being made in
Bexley, which will be invaluable in the future.

This sense of a bigger picture, and of the importance of a shared set of
objectives, will become ever-more pertinent as the implications of the
schools white paper take hold. With local authorities moving towards
commissioning roles, and extended schools commissioning after-
hours provision, leaders will need to learn to give up some power
if they are to coordinate a range of different services successfully. For
example, leaders will need to find ways of using the commissioning
process itself to draw together different providers and agree a
shared set of objectives. This may be through adopting inclusive
commissioning processes that draw on a range of different

perspectives, or it may be through actively shaping the market in order that it works towards long-term, holistic outcomes, rather than bounded and short-term efficiency, which simply stores up problems for other services to deal with.

Use structures to send clear signals

Leaders also stressed the need to make it clear that they are serious about the changes they are making in their organisations. This is one of the ways that structural change can be helpful: rather than seeing new structures as instruments of change, themselves, leaders used the process of restructuring to highlight a problem – and to send a message of the changes needed in a local area.

While it is easy to characterise the use of symbols as a 'soft' approach to leadership, the children's services agenda itself offers a clear example of the ripple effect that such symbols can create, whether they are intended or not (see box 5). The vast majority of the early appointments of directors of children's services were drawn from education backgrounds, despite the lack of any formal suggestion that directors of education should be considered more qualified for the job than their counterparts in social services. However, these early appointments were made against a background in which the minister for children had been located in the Department for Education and Skills, and Ofsted – the Office for Standards in Education – had been appointed as the lead inspectorate for children's services.

Box 5 Case study: The use of symbolic changes

One leader in a local authority explained to us that she had made symbolic changes to structures within the senior management team to send a decisive message to the rest of the staff, both about the leadership team's commitment to the changeover and also about the nature of the changes themselves. Making her management team interdisciplinary communicated that the overarching outcome of the shift was to close gaps within the existing service provision.

People saw that we were serious because we put it into practice at the highest level.

Leaders of extended schools are already taking on this lesson – with many headteachers deliberately choosing to locate social workers, police and other professionals on school grounds, as a way of sending a clear message to pupils, parents and staff. The new not-for-profit Trusts envisaged in the white paper may well wish to adopt a similar approach, through appointing professionals from the wider family of children's services to the governing bodies of schools. Similarly, local authorities are guaranteed a place on the governing body of every Trust school – and choosing who they send may be another way of communicating both the school's wider responsibilities and the role of authorities within that.

Having taken these initial steps to work towards addressing the culture of their organisations, several leaders highlighted the importance of understanding the nature of that transition. They emphasised the importance of pacing change appropriately, and of responding in a constructive fashion to those who are reluctant to alter working practices instantaneously. These issues are the focus of the following chapter.

5. Facing the change

The leaders we spoke to during our research spoke of the need to be able to interpret and respond to the different explanations for negativity and reluctance to change. The changes to children's services have prompted different responses in professionals and users throughout the system and have not been unconditionally positive. Despite broad support, there are reservations about 'teachers becoming social workers' or professionals becoming 'jacks of all trades'. Moreover, the challenges of introducing initiatives such as extended schools illustrate that while changes may be embraced in theory, people often find themselves less sure when it becomes another concern in their own, over-crowded professional lives.[32]

Different rates of change

The leaders we spoke to understood that people engaged with change at different rates and in different ways. They tried to give legitimate opportunities for people to express reservations. People also spoke about how difficult it is when workers are apparently being asked to reverse changes they've spent a long time introducing.

In some cases, people feel they're being asked to reverse their life's work. It's not surprising they have trouble with that.

In the end, I had to leave [the authority]. I felt that I couldn't bear to watch as they undid so much of the work that I'd spent

three years building up. I understood their reasons for doing it –
and it wasn't a bad idea – it would just have been too difficult to
be the person leading those changes.

The youth green paper has inspired similarly confused and unsure
reactions from some professionals in the youth service. Having first
struggled to co-exist with Connexions in the first part of its
implementation, youth workers are now facing another set of changes
that will potentially engender more shifts in relationships between
statutory youth services, Connexions, schools and other provision
directed towards young people.

This attempt to differentiate between the various reactions to
change is an idea borne out in the literature. Studies have shown that
people fall into several categories in response to being presented with
a new idea, or a suggestion of change. Some will instantly embrace the
idea, perhaps because they think it is excellent, or because they are the
type of people that consistently embrace new approaches. Others will
progressively accept the change – at different rates, depending on the
propensity to accept new thinking and their distance from the
original focal point of the innovation. Just over half of most people
are usually in this category. A final minority will refuse to accept the
change at all and will resolutely reject it from their practice.[33]

Leaders have a crucial role to play in understanding these different
responses to change. For the whole 'middle band' of change
acceptance – those that will accept it eventually but don't do so
immediately – there is a period when they appear to be one of the
'cynics' – those that will never accept the change. But leaders need to
model a response that recognises that most people move out of that
phase eventually, with only a minority remaining there for good.

Change and professionalism

Leaders also recognised that sometimes people's resistance to change
was actually connected to their professionalism. This is especially true
for public services. Through their work, teachers, social workers and
their colleagues are regularly in a position to make decisions or offer

services that can change the direction of children's lives. Often, their reported professional preference is to be able to do this in a relatively stable environment, without coping with other professional upheavals or changes in personnel.

Sometimes it seems that the best heads and leaders are those who manage to cope with the barrage of policies targeted at them without losing sight of the core purpose of their organisation.

When major change is introduced, professionals in vital services have a twin set of concerns. First, will the nature of the changes have positive consequences for the children and families for whom they work? Will they improve outcomes for their service users? But, second, will the process of change actually present a threat to service delivery itself? During the period in which professionals are acclimatising to new working arrangements, are things much more likely to go wrong?

These concerns are legitimate and the people that have them are often reflecting the best of the values that we would hope to find in people working in these services. At a time when people are highly critical of the commitment and quality of work of people in social services in particular, anxieties about change could actually be interpreted as a reassuring signal – an indication that professionals are deeply engaged with the core purposes of their work and are sceptical of another set of reforms being brought in.

Again, these leaders' tolerant approach to sceptics is reflected in the literature about change. Senge argues that delivering a change does not have to amount to getting complete agreement from all members of the organisation. He distinguishes between commitment, enrolment and compliance.[34] Although ideally everyone would be committed, that isn't vital to achieve progress. Rather, people go through various stages of engagement (from apathy and non-compliance through to formal compliance, enrolment and then commitment) and it is possible to work with people from the point when they become formally compliant, although less productively than if they are committed. Leaders of children's services respect colleagues at all stages of accepting the change and earn their support over time.

These insights have two main implications:

1. Pacing change at the appropriate rate is crucial.
2. Leaders must find ways to assuage fears and generate impetus for change elsewhere in their organisations.

Pacing change

Several leaders agreed that pacing change in organisations is crucial, particularly given the natural tendency for cynicism that we have just described. The guidance around children's services has successfully incorporated some of what we know about the dangers of forcing change through faster than is achievable, as well as the potential for lasting transformation over a long time. For example, those authorities required to produce a CYYP have until April 2006 to do so, while considerable lead-in time was given to putting directors of children's services in place. A decade is frequently suggested as the timescale during which we will see real impact of the rearrangements happening now.

This point becomes particularly important in relation to engendering large-scale cultural change. Leaders we spoke to highlighted that the timeframe for those sorts of shifts was lengthy.

> Realistically, we're talking years before the way that people think starts to permanently change.

Responding appropriately to people's recalcitrant responses to change can actually help to ensure that they move to acceptance more quickly than if they were criticised. Leaders of children's services were prepared to have difficult conversations about the way to bring in change and, when they can, make discussions about the strategies for moving forward open, transparent and inclusive.[35]

A leader who doesn't listen is a walking disaster area . . . I hate
charismatic leaders . . . there's often a lot of grunge underneath
. . . it's not the charismatic head that will lead them . . . it's the
person who asks them what they want.

This point is made persuasively by Ronald Heifetz in *Leadership*
Without Easy Answers. Heifetz summarises his argument by drawing
on a remark made by the American President Lyndon Johnson:
'Congress is like a whiskey drinker. You can put an awful lot of
whiskey in a man if you let him sip it. But if you try and force the
whole bottle down his throat at one time he'll throw it up.'[36] Leaders
can influence cultural change, but rarely can they force it.

Conversely, while the five needs identified in *Every Child Matters*[37]
embodied ideas around which a range of professionals could come
together, the reality of breaking down needs into specific targets
has sometimes brought in the familiar conflicts over different areas
of responsibility. As a result, people's initial motivation can be
diminished.

It can be hard for people to keep going when there are initial
disappointments.

But the period in which people become discouraged can also be the
period in which the relentless innovation of the early stages ends and
the successful practices can start to take hold and spread more
effectively throughout a system.[38] As a result, over longer periods,
new innovations are far more successful than might have been first
imagined, and there is less opposition. In short, our frustrations in
the short term often lead us to underestimate what is possible in the
long term.[39]

Several leaders described their role as buffers between short
termism and the longer-term, real gains that come from a sustained
commitment to a particular set of changes.

> *I should be the person who manages people's expectations about how quickly a real change will be possible.*

This is an approach reflected in the literature around leadership and management. One study investigating leaders of successful social initiatives found that success came when the individuals held a long-term commitment to the project itself, accompanied by the capacity to adapt to challenges as they emerge in the operating environment.[40]

Similarly, research on change within the NHS has highlighted the use of 'readiness and capability' approaches, which identify key advocates of a change early on in the process and then monitor and build their readiness and ability to introduce the change – an approach also used in larger-scale opinion-forming exercises.[41] Making sure there are a few 'quick wins' – small, early and highly tangible success stories – can also buoy morale during periods of frustration.[42] By using these strategies, leaders can reduce the speed and the extent to which people are disappointed with the initial progress of a new project.

These insights may well hold some important lessons for leaders in local and central government as Children's Trusts move towards a commissioning role in local services. The temptation for policy-makers is to regard the move towards a new system of governance as an immediate substitution of one set of outcomes for another. However, as with the delivery of children's services in the past, the implications of the changes being made at the moment will take time to emerge. In particular, if leaders are able to adopt approaches to contracting that build incentives for providers to bring services together around prevention and early intervention, then the benefits of this approach will only be felt in the medium to long term.

Assuaging people's fears

Beyond straightforward patience, borne out of the recognition that most of the cynics will come round in the end, leaders reflected on the importance of finding practical ways of addressing professionals' concerns in order to help generate changes in culture. The evaluation of the Children's Trust pathfinders found that a key factor in generating support for changes in practice was the 'perception of successful joint working between agencies'.[43]

Through mandating small groups to pilot new approaches, leaders can help actually demonstrate to professionals that a new approach is workable in practice. Furthermore, this can also help to generate other voices in a local area that are positive about the prospect of widespread change. Particularly when people in these working groups are drawn together from different parts of an organisation, their enthusiasm for a new approach that has been discovered or tested out can be infectious when they return to work in their original positions. In this way leaders can escape the trap of having to drag their organisations through periods of change, through creating a cadre of leaders in the ranks.

A key characteristic of these approaches also seems to be what David Hargreaves describes as 'disciplined innovation'.[44] As we have argued, people can become overwhelmed when ask to face up to too much change or experimentation at any given moment, and can easily retreat back into familiar professional habits that can make transition even more difficult. Through sharing the load for new approaches between different groups, or cross-cutting networks, leaders can help overcome this difficulty (see box 6).

> **Box 6 Case study: The use of small, cross-cutting groups**
>
> One director explained that in her organisation a small inter-professional group had been mandated to pursue innovation across the local authority, testing different strategies for addressing issues that were particularly challenging. They took ideas from all levels of the organisation and funded and monitored their progress.
>
> *When an idea works we look at ways to roll it out across the whole of [the authority]. Because it has been tested we aren't asking people to take a complete leap of faith. But it's also still innovative enough to give people a boost and make them feel they're part of something exciting.*

In children's centres and extended schools, leaders are already finding ways of using small-scale experimentation to help challenge received wisdom and introduce new cultural norms. Similarly, the introduction of different commissioning arrangements in the schools white paper has the potential to increase the importance of this approach. It is vital for the broadening of provision implied in the paper that local authorities take a lead in shaping the forces which govern the nature of the providers that thrive from the change in arrangements; it is critical that they do not believe themselves to be passive in the face of market development.

But, equally, to justify the particular 'shape' that they seek out, they will have to test not only specific relationships with particular organisations, but also the nature of those relationships themselves. Small groups innovating around commissioning arrangements, as well as being responsible for commissioning new and innovative services, could hold the key to giving local authorities a significant stake in developing the landscape of providers in the long term.

Finding ways of testing and then demonstrating the validity of new approaches can, therefore, help assuage people's fears around new ways of working. However, the leaders we spoke to described this as part of a wider process of freeing professionals and overcoming disproportionate concerns surrounding risk management. We address this issue directly in the next chapter.

6. Risking it

It's a live laboratory, really. Children are at risk and schools could go down the pan.

Many of the issues that we discussed in the last chapter are intimately connected to the issue of risk. For example:

O Professionals worry about the risks induced by experimentation in their everyday practice.
O People can be reluctant to take on wider responsibilities, and work outside professional boundaries.
O The objective judgement of professionals is regarded as less risk-laden than the subjective preferences of young people.

Each of these risks is rightly factored in to professional judgements in an environment in which mistakes can have tragic consequences. The nature of children's services, however – high stakes, emotive public responses to failures to protect or young people, demands for someone to be held accountable – can in itself create a further risk. This is the risk that services are distorted as professionals resort to managing their own reputations.

As Mike Power has argued, this tendency can have very serious consequences;[45] it can lead to what he describes as the 'risk management of everything' – where process-driven risk management overrides professional judgement – and can prevent organisations from learning from the past as mistakes are covered up. Both of these tendencies can seriously damage the quality of services that children and young people receive.

In response to these problems, the leaders that we spoke to highlighted the importance of identifying creative ways to determine and manage risk, while continuing to push the boundaries of what can be achieved. Two key ways in which this can be achieved are through:

O   reconsidering risk
O   creating safe spaces for learning.

Reconsidering risk

Leaders in children's services were very conscious that one of the keys to making successful inroads into children's services would require them to take a strong position on risk.

> *Risk management is a big thing . . . people are very frightened by risk management.*

By amalgamating social services with other aspects of children's services delivery, local authorities will now be addressing the issue of risk to children in a more joined-up way, rather than within the silos of single areas of provision. But mixing universal services with those designed primarily to reach those deemed to be 'at risk' will lead to new challenges for local authorities trying to find a consistent approach to addressing and managing risk.

> *Dealing with blending a universal service – like schools – with a service that's often caught up with crisis interventions – like social services – has been a real challenge. A lot of that is about risk.*

Managing risk in organisations with non-profit-making aims can also bring additional difficulties. Risks emerge as a result of being driven almost exclusively by minimising the chance of accident and, in so doing, losing sight of the core purpose of an organisation's activity. Most frequently, these risks are connected to the values of the organisation in question and tend to be experienced acutely by organisations with motives other than profit.

Conversations about risk become difficult, because they are focused around issues to do with children's lives,

Essentially, risk is experienced at three levels within an organisation:

1. *Personal*: something bad could happen to a user of the service or to a member of staff. This includes child deaths, but also workers coming to physical harm while doing their job.
2. *Professional*: by making a mistake, an individual worker could be accused of negligence and may lose their job, or be demoted or suspended as a result of it.
3. *Organisational*: the reputation or operating capacity of the organisation as a whole may be affected, either as a result of a 'real' problem, such as financial mismanagement across a number of departments, or due to perceived incompetence, perhaps as a result of media interest in a particular incident.

It seems that the best approaches to managing risk take into account these risks in an overarching sense, rather than viewing them as being unrelated to one another. In particular, this means thinking about the risks of not doing the best for each child, as well as risks associated with preventing the worst.

There are risks associated with being so worried about bad things which might happen that we get separated from our core purpose as professionals, which is to give children a good and happy childhood that sets them up to move into adult life on a good foundation.

Only by considering risk as it applies to all areas of children's lives – the 'risk' of not engaging in school, or the 'risk' of having discontinuities in relationships with adult professionals – will system leaders be in a position to take a clear line on managing risk within the new Trusts. Recognising that there are risks associated with overly restricted opportunities, for example, a stunted sense of independence for a child on the verge of adolescence, is central to providing the best services to vulnerable and mainstream children.

Dealing with risk will be a challenge for the new services, but it is a chance to reconsider the way we tackle these issues.

They will be engaging not only with risk as it applies to the particular period of transition that children's services are entering, but also with the opportunities to reconsider the way that risk is viewed in the system overall.

Creating safe spaces for learning

Leaders can help overcome the tendency for professionals to resort to managing the risk to their own reputations by creating safe spaces for learning inside their organisations. To an extent, the tactic of mandating small groups of innovators can help to achieve this. The value of these groups is that they can be explicitly charged with learning on behalf of the organisation, shifting perceptions from 'delivery' to a more forward-thinking approach.

The language of experimentation and learning can create nervousness when applied to children and young people but, again, there is a creeping risk of the failure to innovate: the prospect of services that never find new solutions to seemingly intractable problems. In this way, the statement: 'Every year of failure represents a lost year in the life of a child, and blights their future'[46] is not an argument for playing it safe in every given situation. Rather, the challenge for leaders is to ensure that these safe spaces for learning are equally safe for young people. This must involve a set of non-negotiable or minimum standards which are applied to help ensure the well-being of the child in question.

Notwithstanding these non-negotiables, however, there are other ways in which leaders can help establish safe spaces for learning in, through building working practices into people's everyday routines. The After Action Review undertaken by the US army is a frequently cited example of this.[47] After a mission open meetings are held, in a blame-free atmosphere, where officers of all ranks are expected to contribute to answering three key questions:

O   What was the aim of the mission?
O   What actually happened?
O   What accounts for the difference?

Applying similar basic texts to situations where support for a child has been inadequate, or after a particularly 'near miss', or even cases which have gone especially well, seems to have the potential to create a lasting impact on the way in which services are delivered. Box 7 offers a case study of this in a number of US nursing units.

> ### Box 7 Case study: Creating open cultures of learning
>
> In the early 1990s, researchers from Harvard Business School were shocked by the findings of what they had expected to be a routine study of eight nursing units in hospitals in the United States. To their surprise, they found that the most effective units that they studied appeared to be making up to ten times the number of errors as the least effective.
>
> What eventually emerged from the study was that, in fact, the most successful units were not more prone to accidents – they were just more likely to report them. And this willingness to be open about mistakes allowed those units to learn from mistakes and improve their performance in the future. By contrast, the less

successful units were hamstrung by a blame culture which prevented such open dialogue, producing stagnation rather than continual improvement.

The conclusion of Amy Edmondson, the lead researcher on the project, was that professionals must feel 'psychologically safe' in organisations before they can be expected to discuss their mistakes with colleagues and superiors.

Of course, it is far easier to write about creating open cultures of learning than it is to create them – ingrained patterns of behaviour cannot always simply be overcome by the protestations of a leader that no one will be blamed. This is even more the case in children's services, where feelings can run extremely high. Therefore, as part of the process of helping large-scale cultural shifts take place, leaders must look for opportunities to create spaces for learning that do not rely merely on the willingness of professionals to break with the norm and risk their reputation.

This provides an opportunity to learn from an established practice in the NHS: the reporting of critical incidents. These incidents (or 'significant event audits') are events which have caused, or could have caused, an adverse outcome to a patient or member of staff. An example of a critical incident might be a misdiagnosis or a drug error. Incidents are reported anonymously online, protecting the confidentiality of both the person doing the reporting and of anyone who may have been involved in the incident itself. Critical incidents are then reviewed by teams, to feed back the lessons into people's working practices. This process is designed to offer an opportunity for personal reflection, but also a way 'to highlight the learning needs of individuals or the team and then incorporate this learning into everyday practice'.[48]

This practice is a significant step in helping to find a way around the natural temptation to cover up mistakes in organisations. Through systematically creating these safe spaces in children's services, leaders may be able to help professionals move towards a situation where the reporting of low-profile errors becomes the norm, and where open discussions become far more of a realistic option.

Some of these practices for managing risk have already been adopted in individual elements of children's services. In some authorities, they may be familiar to professionals across the children's services remit. But the introduction of the *Every Child Matters* legislation is critical to the way we address risk, not least in that it formally marries services that are universal in character with those that work primarily with children with very particular needs, often those in crisis.

This provides an opportunity to stop and take stock of some of the overarching trends in risk management – away from professional judgement, and towards process, for instance – that may not add value to the delivery of services overall. More practically, it also presents us with an opportunity to draw together the different cultural approaches to risk in different facets of children's services and bring them together to create a shared baseline of expectations that will prevent children from slipping through the gaps.

7. The next generation

As the tasks of leadership change, so too must our expectations of who the best candidates for leadership positions really are. As we suggested in chapter 3, we often look for strong or visionary leaders, particularly in times of stress, but many of the highly effective leaders that we met did not conform to this stereotype. The task of cultural change is more subtle that this. More often than not, what we saw was notable humility on the part of leaders, in eschewing the temptation to regard change in very personal terms.

However, the way in which we progress in organisations is through glorifying our own achievements. As one police officer told us:

> The nearer I get to the top, the more I have to unlearn most of the things that got me here.

This has serious implications for the decisions that leaders of children's services make when settling on who to promote. The danger is that we promote the leaders who are, in fact, least well equipped to succeed in the delicate art of changing cultures within organisations. Particularly as managerial power is substituted by an emphasis on commissioning and coordination for local authorities, children's services will need leaders who are capable of opening up discussion between different service providers, rather than closing it down.

It's important not always to go for the most obvious person when you're giving a promotion. People who have the confidence of their colleagues, perhaps more so than their superiors, are often undervalued.

This is particularly important when it is recognised that an important task for leaders is identifying and pursuing succession strategies for themselves.

For people in leadership of children's services, the next few years in post will be particularly challenging, as the first wave of innovations associated with the change are brought into being. In many cases, leaders who establish a particular project, or who see an organisation through an especially difficult time, become very closely associated with an organisation's identity. At times, taking over from these individuals can be extremely challenging for a successor.[49]

But for the longevity of children's services, as well as creating sustainable working environments for staff, it is vital that leaders find strategies for ensuring they are supported and ultimately succeeded by highly competent individuals. Most of the leaders interviewed were pragmatic about changing jobs after a period of time in their present role.

I'm only here for five years . . . that was the arrangement from the point when I joined.

In many cases, Children's Trusts confront difficult issues in recruiting to leadership posts. First, in many authorities former colleagues have competed for the director's role, leading to difficulties when only one person is appointed (or perhaps neither of the internal candidates). Second, local authority employment protocols make it problematic if someone is seen to be being 'anointed' for a particular post – it can be interpreted as an unacceptable sort of professional 'favouritism' that can sometimes seem to have implicit other, less acceptable, criteria for selection.

Third, the individuals that make the best leaders during periods of major change may not end up being comparable to those who make good leaders during times when things need to be kept stable – during the years when the changes made now will become embedded in people's practice. But creating opportunities to build the capacity for succession within local authorities is vital, as reflected in IDeA's Skills Framework for Elected Members which, among other things, suggests that members should 'empower others to take responsibility' and 'take a long-term view in developing networks and partnerships' and embrace practical applications of those ideas, such as Haringey's member development programme.[50]

Recent trends in new legislation also suggest that the field for potential recruits will only become more varied. As more and more non-local authority providers become involved with the delivery of services as a result of the schools white paper, leaders with a range of experience will become increasingly important. The net will need to be cast wide for those to fill leadership roles, to ensure that new recruits have an understanding of a cross-section of organisations and experiences.

Senge identifies people's attachment to their particular roles, or positions, as one of his 'organisational learning disabilities'.[51] He argues that when people see themselves exclusively in terms of their position within an organisation, they filter what they hear and see in terms of that role, which diminishes the value of their perceptions. People develop behaviours that 'match' their position, rather than developing from their own starting point to engage with their role.

Leaders need to create a framework in which their colleagues feel confident to experiment, provide genuine feedback and learn from mistakes. This won't be easy in every organisation, as Binney and Williams explain:

> It feels uncomfortable, particularly for leaders in organisations where this style is not the norm. It requires a high degree of self-belief and a willingness to try.[52]

Equally, this sort of capacity building can also demand looking beyond the immediate boundaries of organisations, with leaders brokering relationships with other organisations that may be closer to the particular issue.[53] Central to this is retaining an open mind about who should be recruited or promoted. People who consistently present themselves as being key to an organisation's success, or achieving above and beyond their colleagues and peers, may not be the best people to be honest about the learning that they, as well as others, will have to do during a period of change. Being prepared to be seen to be wrong in public is often not easy for candidates who pursue success by presenting near-perfection to their colleagues and superiors. Good leaders during transition periods will often need to be humble, and publicly so.

I see it as my job as a leader to ask the silly questions . . . to find out about the things that people feel embarrassed to ask about and to get to the bottom of things that people might make assumptions about.

In addition, leaders need to be prepared to engage with a broader definition of what constitutes 'succession'. For some organisations, a successful leader may eventually make themselves redundant, through building diverse and effective relationships with other organisations, including those from private and voluntary sectors. Equally, succession can be understood in terms of the system as a whole, rather than exclusively within particular leadership posts and roles within existing organisational structures.

Applying principles that create less hierarchical organisations can help to build a foundation for people moving into leadership later on in their careers. 'Business process reengineering', for instance, advocates shifting organisations away from giving people very straightforward tasks as individuals and towards teams of workers focusing on all the aspects of a particular challenge.[54] As a result, it is argued, leaders' roles will move from supervising and keeping score, to coaching and genuine leadership (see box 8).

> ### Box 8 Case study: Rewarding team players
>
> The sandwich firm Prêt à Manger works hard to avoid a situation in which success is overly personalised. When anyone is promoted in one of the stores, they are given a sum of money to award to the people that they feel have helped them achieve their promotion. Aside from incentivising a more cooperative approach within the firm, this also sends a clear signal – that we often owe our success to others.
>
> This emphasis on mutual interdependence is reinforced by the company's recruitment procedures. Prospective employees are asked to work for a day in a shop before they are taken on. At the end of the day, existing staff take a vote on whether the new employee should be hired not. If the vast majority don't vote in favour, then the candidate doesn't get the job.

Each of these areas has a profound effect on the way in which children's services are shaped and delivered at a local level. Equally, however, the national policy context can be responsible for helping or hindering the extent to which progress is made locally. The next two chapters will examine what the local changes in children's services could mean for the national policy picture.

8. The national picture: part 1

Thus far we have argued that leadership at the local level will be vital in determining the long-term success of the proposed changes to children's services. The fundamental changes that professionals are being asked to deliver will require considerable shifts in culture if children's services are not to drift back in to the comfort zone of old ways of working.

Yet while the incentive of local leaders will be vital in bringing about genuine and long-lasting change, there is another key factor which cannot be ignored. Though the government rightly describes '150 local change programmes' across the country,[55] each of these exists within a national context. In particular, the framework of regulation, strategic planning and advice which central government uses to negotiate objectives and budgets with the local state, especially local authorities, has a crucial influence on the possibilities within each local area. Much of the 'control' exercised by national government over local services takes this form – by requiring plans, outcome measures and specific forms of compliance in return for funding. For this reason, the role of central government in providing strategic leadership in children's services will be discussed in this and the next chapter:

o   This chapter discusses the role of advice and compliance

    from central government in determining the operating
    environment for local leaders.
O   The next chapter looks specifically at accountability
    frameworks.

As we have already suggested, an overriding challenge for leaders at the local level is to create a greater degree of coherence between different services at a time when the providers of children's services are becoming increasingly diverse and self-governing. The recent schools white paper proposes that the term 'local education authority' be removed from the statute book, to signal a shift in emphasis towards a broader role in local governance, but if authorities are to move from being managers of the education system to coordinating hubs in local areas, then the relationship between central and local government must also be re-appraised.

To its credit, central government has acknowledged its role in making this process far simpler for local leaders, through the rationalisation of funding streams and accountability frameworks. It is clear from our research that these are priorities shared by those in local government, and are rightly being pursued, along the lines of the 'onion' shown in figure 2, developed by the Department for Education and Skills.[56]

However, in spite of this determination to provide more coherent and strategic leadership from the centre, problems persist in translating the rhetorical commitment into action. In particular, local efforts to bring about coherence in services are being seriously undermined by the disproportionate number of advisers that are assigned from central government. The list shown in table 1, a collection of all the advisers working with one of the local authorities involved in our research, helps illustrate this problem.

This issue is already subject to scrutiny from central government, under the auspices of the Future Role of Government Offices programme. The comprehensive performance assessment (CPA) process for local authorities is also due to be replaced in the next two to three years, with a performance framework for local government

Figure 2 Onion diagram – model of a Children's Trust

Source: Department for Education and Skills

designed to encourage greater self-evaluation and self-improvement.

In other words, central government recognises the need for coherence, streamlining and integration, and is working incrementally towards a position which seeks to encourage much greater flexibility at a local level, without lowering expectations or accountability. This is very much the thrust of the latest school reform proposals, and a similar emphasis is visible in several other policy areas. But despite the intention, the *approach used* makes a huge difference to the eventual outcome. Government must avoid a

Table 1 List of advisers working with one local authority

Programme	Title and unit
Performance Assessment Framework	Business Relationship Manager, CSCI
Teenage Pregnancy	Regional Adviser, Teenage Pregnancy Unit, DfES
Children's Fund	Development Officer, Sure Start Unit, DfES
Early Years	Strategic Development Officer, Sure Start Unit, DfES
Early Years	Regional Director, Foundation Stage, DfES
Early Years	NNI Regional Adviser
Early Years	Sure Start Finance and Monitoring Programme Developer, DfES
Young People's Substance Misuse	Regional Adviser, Drugs Team
CAHMS	Regional Development Worker, National CAHMS Support Service, DoH
YOT	Regional Adviser, Drugs Team
Children's Trust	Children's Trust Regional Development Adviser, DfES
Integrated Children's System	Regional Development Adviser, DfES
Change for Children	Regional Change Adviser, DfES
Healthy Schools Programme	Regional Coordinator, Health Development Agency
National Remodelling Team	Regional Adviser, NRT
Education	Children's Services Improvement Adviser, DfES
Education Officer	Education Officer, Regional Government Office
Primary Education Strategy	Primary Strategy Regional Adviser, DfES
Key Stage 3 Strategy	Senior Regional Director, DfES Key Stage 3 English Key Stage 3 Maths Key Stage 3 Science ICT Foundation Studies Behaviour and Attendance

'rationalisation' process that works from the perspective of central government, but changes little for local authorities, and which needs to be repeated in a few years' time. Some underlying problems must be tackled, rather than merely redressing the current situation temporarily. This is more than a tidying-up exercise; it is a question of moving away from a standardised system based on the principles of command and control, and towards a more flexible and responsive approach to advice and accountability. Achieving this depends on finding a method of planning and coordination which can be used by local authorities to promote integration *and* innovation across their local area, under the new conditions of diversity and flexibility brought about by children's services and education reforms.

To achieve this, two main issues need to be addressed: first, the unhelpful conflation of advice and compliance under the present arrangements; second, the cumbersome and supply-driven way that advisers are currently assigned to authorities.

Untangling advice and compliance

As we noted in table 1, across a wide range of activities and policy goals, resourcing national funding comes with an 'adviser' attached. The key point here is the serious damage to the relationship between central and local government that is being caused by the present lack of clarity surrounding these 'advisory' roles. As it stands, many roles combine advice and performance management, meaning that authorities can feel unsure whether they are being advised or monitored at any given moment.

This can often lead to a distinctly uncommunicative relationship between central and local government. One leader in a local authority told us that they had become so exasperated that they had simply decided to stop meeting anyone from central government at all.

This lack of clear delineation can serve to close down discussion between central and local government, leading to the development of defensive, or even adversarial, relationships between the two. Such a situation bears a striking resemblance to the 'parallel conversations' that are described by Daniel Goleman in his discussion of the dysfunctional relationships that can develop in a marriage.[57] Goleman suggests that, in reality, dialogue between a husband and a wife often involves *two* conversations rather than one – the spoken conversation and what they both really mean. He argues that these 'parallel conversations' can poison a marriage, leading to a situation where an unspoken war of attrition can become self-confirming. Even positive acts can be interpreted in negative ways, as each partner constantly scans the actions of the other. Box 9 offers an excerpt in which Goleman depicts these parallel 'conversations'.

Box 9 Parallel conversations[58]

The children are being rambunctious, and Martin, their father, is getting annoyed. He turns to his wife, Melanie, and says in a sharp tone, 'Dear, don't you think the kids could quiet down?'

His actual thought: 'She's too easy on the kids.'

Melanie, responding to his ire, feels a surge of anger. Her face grows taut, her brows knit a frown, and she replies, 'The kids are having a good time. Anyhow, they'll be going to bed soon.'

Her thought: 'There he goes again, complaining all the time.'

Martin is now visibly enraged. He leans forward menacingly, his fists clenched, as he says in an annoyed tone, 'Should I put them to bed now?'

His thought: 'She opposes me in everything. I'd better take over.'

Melanie, suddenly frightened by Martin's wrath says meekly, 'No, I'll put them to bed right away.'

Her thought: 'He's getting out of control – he could hurt the kids. I'd better give in.'

This state of affairs can have only negative consequences for children and young people. Though constructive debate between professionals may be a healthy part of organisational life, an ongoing war of attrition between central and local government is not. Central government is entitled, of course, to require that local authorities should meet performance targets and report on their progress in key areas of policy. But building separate reporting lines which develop into 'improvement' activities and relationships does not have to be an inevitable consequence of such requirements. As a first step, **central government should seek to separate the two functions of advice and compliance.** This would help lay the foundations for a far more honest set of conversations in the future, by eliminating the need for central government and authorities to resort to the kind of covert game playing described above. Under this system, a clear separation of the advisers and performance managers would replace the current mixture.

Bespoke systems of advice

This separation of the advice and compliance functions would open up an opportunity to address the second issue that is so evident in the list of advisers in table 1: fragmentation. As is immediately clear from the list, advisers are currently assigned according to the organisational logic of the DfES, and other departments, rather than according to the needs of local authorities. The Teenage Pregnancy Unit sends an adviser, as does the Surestart Unit, as does the Primary Strategy team and the Change for Children team. The result of this is that authorities can be left to deal with an inordinate number of advisers, whose roles may either overlap or simply get in the way of each other.

The first implication of this situation is that it can become a very inefficient use of time and resources, as authorities struggle to manage various different relationships simultaneously. Perhaps more worryingly, though, it can also seriously damage the credibility of those charged with the important role of offering strategic advice and transferring best practice between authorities. As authorities become more and more exasperated with requests for meetings from representatives with central government, the temptation is to brand all contact with 'outsiders' unhelpful. Just as the unspoken battle of wills within a marriage can become self-confirming, so too can valuable advice be lost in the fallout of this breakdown in communication.

Again, it is important not to lose sight of the fact that this institutional malaise can have direct consequences for the life chances of young people. Organisations that are unable to function effectively lose their capacity to meet the complex and constantly changing needs of young people.

Third, the problems that arise from this approach unnecessarily undermine the *valid* case for investment in the life chances of children and young people. Innovations in policy and investment in new services can too easily be dismissed as 'additional bureaucracy' when the system of children's services is not programmed to deal with the complexity that these developments can bring with them. In short, there is a *political* as well as a practical case for rethinking the logic of the current system.

With advice and compliance separated, then, there is no reason why the allocation of advice should happen in a supply-driven fashion, meaning that such problems could be avoided. Authorities could commission advisers from central government if and when they need them. To this end, **budgets for strategic advice should be devolved to the local level, allowing authorities to commission advice from central government or others if and when they need them.** This does not imply that local authorities could simply pick and choose which performance goals or statutory requirements they needed to improve or report against, but that their general duty to improve performance in ways that meet their various specific commitments can be met in a more flexible range of ways. If this could be achieved local authorities would have a much stronger incentive both to integrate their various planning processes and to make more effective use of the resources currently devoted to inspection, 'advice' and compliance activities.

In this situation, it may be that exactly the same number of advisers are commissioned, but the important difference would be that the system would work on the terms of those responsible for commissioning and coordinating services: local authorities. This change would also help address the question of advisers' credibility, by preventing the situation in which they arrive unwelcome in authorities, and simply are ignored as a result. Further, this would apply some of the logic of contestability to central government itself. The DfES and other departments would retain a competitive advantage, having authored the policies themselves, but authorities would be free to commission advice from each other or from the private sector if they saw fit.

One reasonable objection to this system might be that a valuable R&D capacity may be lost to the system, as authorities, revelling in their new-found freedom, choose to cut all ties with central government or other local areas. To avoid this situation, **central government should ring-fence an agreed level of funding for authorities to commission advisers, in order to secure continued investment in this area.** As with other areas of government, the principle of earned autonomy could be applied here, with successful authorities afforded greater freedoms.

The precedent for this approach has already been set. The New Deal for Communities regeneration programme sees budgets devolved to a local level for community projects, with money set aside to ensure that necessary professional experience is brought in to bolster community projects. Under that system, there are a number of accredited advisers for community leaders to choose between, providing some degree of quality assurance from the centre. Crucially, though, advisers are brought in *on the terms of local communities.*

From the DfES five-year strategy[59]

We believe that the delivery of this strategy will require a major reform of the DfES. Our vision of the DfES of the future is that it will be:

More strategic
The core role of the department will be to support ministers in providing strategic leadership to the system. That means setting the overall strategic direction and the outcomes that are being sought for children, young people and adults; developing powerful and relevant evidence-based policy; and having the capacity to engage with those in the system so that they understand and share the direction of travel. To achieve this the department is developing a new strategy unit and a more strategic analytical capacity, enabling us to learn from evidence and from international experience.

The corollary of this is that the department itself will do less direct management and direct service delivery. It will increasingly be the 'system designer', setting in place the framework of legislation, incentives, information and funding to make change happen. It will use the guiding principles of this strategy – personalisation and choice, diversity, freedom and autonomy, and stronger partnerships – to underpin its work.

A further step should also be taken to encourage a more constructive set of relationships between central and local government: **central government should take the lead in facilitating a far greater number of secondments between government departments and local authorities.** Sir Michael Bichard, permanent secretary of the then Department for Education and Employment from 1995 to 2001, has identified several shortcomings in the present configuration of the civil service, arguing that all those employed to provide public services should be part of one system of 'public servants'.[60] Encouraging far more secondments would be a useful first step in addressing some of these issues.

More exchanges between central and local government would undoubtedly add to the skills base in both areas of government but, more importantly, an ongoing programme of secondments would be useful in providing a set of *cultural exchanges* between the two. As Jake Chapman has argued, governance systems are best understood not as objective facts, but as complex webs of relationships, which look very different from other positions.[61] Our problems seem very different from the other side of the fence. At present, short-term 'immersion days' take place as a means of addressing this issue, but the danger of these is that flying visits can serve to reinforce, rather than disrupt, some of our assumptions. For leaders in central government to have spent substantial periods of time – six months as a minimum – working in local government (and visa versa) would be of considerable value to the system.

9. The national picture: part 2

The role of inspection

A second important feature of the national context is the use of accountability mechanisms in children's services. While leaders in local areas will be expected to set standards in their own authorities, each local area will be subject to scrutiny through an annual performance assessment (APA)[62] and a joint area review (JAR).[63]

As we suggested in chapter 3, accountability frameworks offer one way in which leaders can set the agenda in their organisations. Funding and official decision-making power may be 'devolved to the front line', but, in reality, this is reflected only as far as accountability frameworks will allow it. The key issue, then, becomes not whether inspection should shape and invigorate children's services, but rather *how* and *to what extent* this should play out in practice.

One important – and widely recognised – implication of this is that, as we move towards more integrated children's services, built around the needs of young people, it will be important that inspection frameworks are themselves coherent. Indeed this will be central to government's ability to monitor and influence how responsibility for the five outcomes of *Every Child Matters* is being shared across professional boundaries. Crucially, therefore, government must ensure that accountability frameworks do not become as fragmented and detached from operational realities as is seen in the list of advisers set out in table 1.

In this way, central government must find a balance between holding Children's Trusts to account on behalf of young people, and creating artificial barriers to the ability of Trusts to be responsive to local needs. The most effective way of achieving this is to ensure that bespoke systems of advice and support are matched by bespoke systems of accountability.

To an extent, the model for this already exists in the new inspection framework for schools,[64] introduced in September 2005. Schools are now inspected largely on the basis of their own self-assessment, meaning that not only are inspectors provided with a useful dataset, but they are also given an important insight into the particular circumstances, achievements, shortcomings and future objectives of the individual school. This means that rather than beginning with a standardised, predetermined set of indicators, inspectors are increasingly able to ground their judgements in the particular state of affairs in every school they visit. Not only will they be assessing the progress of the school against its stated objectives and accountabilities, but they will be evaluating the capacity of the school as an organisation to *form* such objectives in an appropriate way, relate them to its own specific context, and assess its own progress. This kind of capacity is essential to the ability of any organisation to sustain and internalise the process of innovation and improvement.

We must learn from this innovation, if inspection is to succeed in harnessing the complexities of local delivery, rather than simply adding to them. In order to achieve this, **the CYPP must be put at the heart of each local authority's corporate planning process, with accountability assured through the yearly APA, and the more comprehensive JAR every three years.** The CYPP is the point at which national priorities are brought together with an assessment of local need, and this is exactly the function that inspection needs to play. The present situation, where implementation is regarded as a local issue, with 'drivers' established in central government, does not serve this purpose.

Under a revised system, the APA would provide a lighter-touch form of accountability, with the wider-reaching JAR providing a more thorough-going moderation of the CYPP. Every JAR inspection team should therefore be asked to concern itself with three key questions:

- ○ . How successfully has the CYPP been implemented?
- ○ To what extent has the CYPP reflected local need?
- ○ What changes need to be made to keep the CYPP moving forward?

Importantly, moderating inspection through the CYPP would serve to bring the inspection process closer to children and young people themselves. At present, young people have a role to play as the plan is put together, but their input is diluted by the lack of a firm connection between the plan and the process of inspection. The changes that we suggest would help address this issue.

A second advantage of this approach is that it would allow each inspection team to establish some priorities among the 26 national indicators,[65] by drawing on the analysis and commitments made in each CYPP. This will be crucial in ensuring that national indicators support rather than impinge on the ability of Children's Trusts to be responsive to local need. Box 10 illustrates the importance of this.

Box 10 National indicators and local need

Across government, focusing on a predetermined set of national indicators – however logical each indicator may seem in isolation – can produce unintended consequences or distort the delivery of services at a local level:

- ○ In health, an over-emphasis on shortening waiting lists in hospitals and GP surgeries, through the use of performance indicators, can lead to a situation where people are simply left off lists altogether to ensure that 'waiting times' are seen to improve.

O   In policing, national targets are set for robbery, as
     government responds to calls to curb violent crime. However,
     in some local areas burglary is more of a priority for local
     people, leaving leaders in a bind between meeting national
     performance indicators and serving their local communities.

Furthermore, as the guidance for CYPPs states, 'A good CYPP will . . .
evolve over time and initially in some areas may include the
identification of gaps to be addressed in the first year of
implementation.'[66] This means that the CYPP, alongside each Trust's
own self-assessment, would offer a clear and up-to-date foundation
for an inspection process that will genuinely be able to focus on
outcomes for children and young people in a local area.

There are inevitably some implications that arise from this
approach. Principal among these is that the process for signing off
each authority's CYPP would need to be reviewed, as its completion
would effectively set the terms on which an authority would be
inspected in the future. Presently, there is a duty on almost all
authorities to produce a plan, and some stipulations about who to
involve in the process of so doing, but central government plays no
statutory role in validating the final document.[67]

This would have to change if inspection is to be tailored to each
authority. Through making the plan the point at which an evaluation
of local need meets national priorities (and therefore accountability
mechanisms), **the establishment of the plan would be the key
moment for central government to perform the challenge function,
ensuring, as the guidance states, that 'ambitious but realistic targets
are set for improved outcomes, reflecting national as well as local
priorities'.**[68]

The major advantage of this would be to 'clear the decks' and
establish an unambiguous basis for the continuing relationship
between central and local government. The plan – and the acceptance
of it as the basis for challenge and accountability in the future –
would help discipline the assignment of compliance officers to local

government. Performance managers from central government would be assigned according to the specific elements of a Trust's CYPP; each manager would draw their legitimacy not from organisational silos of central government departments, but from a clear vision of how to make progress in each local area. This could also serve as a model for the forthcoming review of the CPA.

Second, all Trusts would be required to produce a CYPP, whereas authorities deemed to be 'excellent' are currently exempt. However, while this might involve some extra work for a small number of authorities, the payoff would certainly be significant, in helping to establish an accountability system capable of reflecting local circumstances, which genuinely contributes to improved services for children and young people.

One objection to this approach might be that it would lose the present focus on outcomes in the process of forging a coherent and bespoke form of inspection for each authority. This is a reasonable concern and would need to be dealt with in the way in which plans were constructed, with steps taken to ensure that the focus on outcomes that is laid out in the guidance for CYPPs is seen through in practice. However, we do not envisage that a focus on outcomes would be any less sharp – more that the process would be better at relating outcomes to each other, establishing priorities and planning against specific contextual factors. Again, the role of central government in signing off the plan would be crucial here in ensuring that the rationale for inspection in the future is clear and focused on outcomes.

Beyond 'joined up' inspection

While it is crucial that accountability frameworks support, rather than undermine, the efforts of local leaders to forge greater coherence between different services, we know that more accurate accountability frameworks are, in themselves, not enough. As we argued in chapter 3, professional cultures have demonstrated their ability to withstand changes to organisational environments too many times to believe this. Equipped with this knowledge, government needs to ensure that accountability mechanisms are capable of supporting cultural as well as structural change if inspection is to 'improve outcomes for children and young people',[69] as government hopes it will.

We know that the shift to more integrated services – with the greater collaboration between different professions that this implies – will require substantial shifts in professional cultures if it is genuinely to take root. Without this, there will always be the tendency for professionals to fall back into the comfort zone of old ways of working, despite the broad support for the theory behind this new way of working. And we also know that such cultural shifts necessarily involve a process of collective *learning*, as leaders seek to shift people's mental models and work to align their professional values. As central government exercises leadership through inspection, then, it will be important that the inspectors play their own role in helping bringing about this widespread change in culture.

The Education Select Committee has already raised questions as to the role of inspection in the improvement cycle for children's services, stating: 'We maintain that for inspection to serve as a lever for improvement, there needs to be a clear process linking inspection findings, communication of these findings to service(s) inspected and suitable intervention to bring about change.'[70] As with the role of government advisers, however, the emphasis must be on *the communication of these findings* – and the terms on which this happens – if they are to have a significant impact on outcomes.

Under present arrangements, every authority's APA is followed by a meeting, chaired by Ofsted and attended by representatives from central government and the local authority in question. The meeting is primarily designed to highlight strengths and weaknesses of provision in the area, and to discuss emerging findings from the assessment, before the final report is followed up through Commission for Social Care Inspection (CSCI) business relationship managers and DfES children's services improvement advisers.[71]

However, as we have seen, the major challenge for leaders in local areas is not to convince people that more coherent and personalised services are a good idea, but to find ways of *translating the theory into practice.* An inspection team which simply demands that services work together more effectively, therefore, seems unlikely to bring about genuine changes in outcomes alone. Presently, improvement advisers are deployed post-inspection, as authorities try to translate the theory into reality, but this runs into the difficulties of credibility and overlap, discussed earlier in this chapter, and limits the scope for ideas to travel.

The government has made clear that the framework for inspection will be kept under constant review, and it should take the opportunity to give the role of inspection in the improvement cycle clearer definition. To this end, **a light-touch APA should be supplemented by a 'right to recall' for local authorities. Just as we have argued that local authorities should be able to commission advice from central government on their own terms, so too should they be able to recall the inspection team –** *after* **the final report has been delivered and published – for a strategy and planning day.**

The 'right to recall' would offer an opportunity for leaders – should they require it – to draw on the experience of inspectors in a far more constructive working environment. With the final report already delivered, the conflation of advice and compliance could again be avoided, allowing a more forward-thinking dialogue to take place. **Having made this change, central government should mandate inspectors to share excellent practice from other authorities in these meetings.** Presently an inspection team visits every local area in the country, yet the knowledge that inspectors acquire through this process is rarely fed directly back into the system.

By involving inspection teams in this way, an enormous resource of knowledge and experience could be mobilised, enabling the national system of children's services to improve continuously over time through drawing on existing practice. Local authorities could avoid each having to constantly reinvent the wheel, and the feedback loop between policy and practice could be shortened significantly.

To complement this process of continual learning in support of culture change, **government should also commit to involving those working in local authorities in the process of inspecting others. As a** minimum, one member of every inspection team should be working elsewhere in a local authority, preferably in the management tier directly below the director of children's services. This approach would have three key benefits.

First, it would aid the process of transferring excellent ideas between local areas, by giving senior members of local authorities the opportunity to visit other local areas, enabling them to draw on the examples of effective practice or management strategies.

Second, it would help build the credibility of inspection teams, in the eyes of those whom they inspect, helping them to play this more strategic role. In our discussion with a number of professionals involved in the design and delivery of children's services, one of the clear themes was that inspectors face the challenge of evaluating a system that leaders may have no direct experience of themselves. Involving at least some degree of peer inspection would help to address this perceived credibility gap.

Third, it would broaden the experience base of the next generation of directors of children's services. As one of our interviewees told us, 'It is one thing to create a new position, but another to find a cadre of leaders with the ability and experience to fill it.' One of the great challenges for directors of children's services is that the role draws together two areas – education and social services – of which they will often have experience of only one.

Until now, career paths have tended to follow either the education or social services route. As the Commission for Social Care Inspection has commented, 'It is essential that the range of skills which the new Directors of Children's Service possess, draw together the experiences of both Directors of Education and Directors of Social Services. It is essential that there is no loss of expertise and knowledge of children's social care.'[72] Therefore, through broadening the experience of the next tranche of leaders through peer inspection, central government could play an important role in supporting the capacity building that we described earlier.

This commitment to using inspection as a means to help support large-scale cultural change in children's services seems particularly apt when applied to the role of schools. The Children Act placed a legal duty to cooperate on strategic bodies only, rather than operational agencies, meaning that schools have found themselves free from such formal obligations.

School inspection

In addition to this, the *Five Year Strategy for Children and Learners*,[73] published last year, and the recent schools white paper,[74] introduced far greater independence of schools from local authorities. The result of this is that while authorities may continue to be regarded as strategic bodies, their ability to direct the affairs of schools looks set to only diminish. Therefore, while schools may have acquired a wider set of responsibilities (to contribute to the well-being of pupils), the traditional 'levers' for ensuring that this takes place are falling in number.

In this situation, it will be important that the new additions to the inspection framework for schools reflect these wider aspirations. Although most professionals agree with the suggestion that 'effective support to respond to children's individual needs outside the classroom will help unlock potential and aspiration inside it',[75] as the white paper suggested, the danger is that the ways in which we measure success encourage excessive focus on one aspect of a child's development alone.

Under the APA, local authorities will fail if they don't achieve sufficient standards in both education and social services, and the same principle should be applied to schools. Just as failure to meet expected levels of academic achievement act as a trigger for Special Measures, so too should consistent failure to address the well-being of children. In the framework that we are proposing, the contribution of individual schools (and of groups of schools and partnerships involving schools) towards community-based outcomes such as well-being would also be much easier to gauge than is currently possible using the standard indicators of school performance.

To compliment this, **schools should also be required, as part of their self-assessment, to assess the quality of their working**

relationships with other service providers. The government may well be reluctant to impose a duty to cooperate on schools, but encouraging an open conversation about the strengths and weaknesses of this aspect of a school's performance should not be shied away from. As with the other professions involved in children's services, however, the greatest challenge is not that teachers need to be forced to engage with other professions, but rather that they must learn *how* to take on this role.

I've been teaching for 35 years but I don't know what happens in social services, but I should do and I'm learning.
Deputy headteacher

The same difficulties of differing professional values and historical separation of roles exist, and the same cultural change will be necessary. As one headteacher commented at a recent conference on extended schools, 'In the past, being a head was like playing football; you knew your position and where you were on the pitch. Today it's more like orienteering; you don't know either of these things so you have to rely on your wits and on other people.'[76]

Therefore, in order to support this process of learning, the changes we suggest to the APA of local authorities could also be reflected in the school inspection framework:

O   The 'right to recall' could be afforded to schools, providing the opportunity for a strategy day after the official report for the school had been published.

O   Inspectors could be made explicitly responsible for transferring excellent practice on these strategy days, allowing schools to learn from each other how to do more and do better simultaneously.

In recent years, the government has spent a considerable amount of time and effort in trying to 'scale up' excellent practice. A range of approaches has been experimented with, including interventions such as the national literacy and numeracy strategies, and initiatives designed to promote networking, such as beacon schools, the Leading Edge Partnership Programme, federations, networked learning communities. Using the latent resource of school inspection teams to help schools learn from one another would be an extremely valuable way of helping schools to do more and to do better simultaneously.

As with local authorities, the success of such an approach would also be dependent on the credibility of the inspection teams involved. And, as we have discussed earlier, credibility depends less on objective facts than it does on people's everyday personal judgements. If inspectors are *seen* to be out of touch, then their judgements are far more likely to be dismissed. To reflect this, two further steps should be taken to support a more ambitious role for school inspection:

○ **Peer inspection could be woven into the Ofsted process, with at least one member of the team having spent at least 60 days a year working in a school.**

○ **Inspection could be tailored to each school, with professionals assigned to schools on the basis of their experience, ensuring that those who had worked in large schools in urban areas were inspecting exactly that type of school.**

Each of these measures would be a significant help to schools as they try to navigate their way through a wider set of responsibilities, and a far greater level of engagement with a number of different professions.

10. Conclusion: the leadership imperative

We have concluded this report with a detailed focus on the arrangements for inspection, regulation and improvement across children's services. This focus stems from our conviction that these arrangements have a crucial influence on the extent to which professionals and providers will be able to achieve the long-term goals of *Every Child Matters* and the Children Act.

Addressing the issues of leadership for children's services also acts as a timely reminder of the importance of leadership throughout the public sector. As we see the process of widespread reform take hold throughout the public services, the lessons learned from the introduction of integrated delivery for children will become pertinent across the full range of provision.

Establishing a new, mutually reinforcing balance between the responsibilities and accountabilities of different players on this field is genuinely possible, if the main players are able to recognise the potential for alignment that comes from innovation in the way that children's services are inspected and regulated.

But the deeper challenge remains the one with which we began: that of establishing a shared direction across increasingly complex systems and communities, which is rooted in an ethical commitment to all children but is capable of challenging and transcending the specific practices and structures currently used by different groups of professionals.

The everyday practice of leadership is central to meeting this challenge, precisely because leadership enables people to take risks and go beyond their familiar practices. In every authority, and probably in every neighbourhood, this shared imperative is likely to create specific opportunities for development – shared learning opportunities across separate organisations, informal networks which involve parents and families in new ways, common approaches to professional learning and workforce development.

Possibly the most concrete opportunity to meet the leadership imperative would be to ensure that the various institutions responsible for supporting leadership development – across local government, health, social services, schools and the voluntary sector – seek shared ways in which to support the development of leadership skills which work effectively across these different worlds. This would not mean seeking to reduce all professions to one, or to create a single set of requirements for senior positions in children's services – but it does mean examining the opportunities for cross-connection and for integrating different leadership curricula and support programmes.

Much simpler, however, and potentially more widespread, is the basic leadership imperative: for all those involved in children's services – from nursery assistants to government ministers – to recognise and legitimise the efforts of those who are trying to overcome the immediate constraints of the context in which they work. Where leadership can do this, it will support their efforts to learn their way into new habits, new methods and new achievements.

Notes

1   T Blair, 'Foreword by the Prime Minister', *Every Child Matters*, green paper (Norwich: HMSO, 2003).

2   Department for Education and Skills, schools white paper, *Higher Standards, Better Schools for All: More choice for parents and pupils* (Norwich: TSO, 2005).

3   *The Victoria Climbié Inquiry: Report of an inquiry by Lord Laming* (Norwich: TSO, 2003).

4   R Adams, L Dominelli and M Payne (eds), *Social Work: Themes, issues and critical debates*, 2nd edn (Basingstoke: Palgrave, 2002).

5   C Leadbeater, *Learning About Personalisation: How can we put the learner at the heart of the education system?* (London: DfES, 2004).

6   M Power, *The Risk Management of Everything* (London: Demos, 2004).

7   J Craig, *Schools Out: Can teachers and social workers learn to live together?* (London: Demos 2004).

8   Learning Working Group, *About Learning* (London: Demos, 2005).

9   See the webpage of the Child Development Institute: www.cdipage.com (accessed 16 Nov 2005).

10 See www.thewhocarestrust.org.uk/ (accessed 16 Nov 2005).

11 M Pedlar, J Burgoyne and T Boydell, *A Manager's Guide to Leadership* (Maidenhead: McGraw-Hill Business, 2004).

12 'Parents say council chiefs must face action', *Independent*, 5 Jun 2005.

13 For example, the death of a child on a Leeds secondary school's trip to France; see: www.nut.org.uk/story.php?id=1949 (accessed 16 Nov 2005).

14 R Heifetz, *Leadership Without Easy Answers* (Cambridge, MA: Harvard University Press, 1994).

15 *Victoria Climbié Inquiry*.

16 T Bentley, *Everyday Democracy* (London: Demos, 2005).

17 Ofcom is a good example of this, where five different regulators have been brought under the same organisational umbrella, leading to genuine improvements to its service.

18   E Mayo, *A Playlist for Public Services* (London: National Consumer Council, 2005).

19   T Bentley, *Letting Go: Complexity, individualism and the Left* (London: Renewal, 2003).

20   www.everychildmatters.gov.uk/_files/ 49856C0DEC294CB7D05131CBCBC418BE.pdf (accessed 16 Nov 2005).

21   www.parliament.the-stationery- office.co.uk/pa/cm200405/cmselect/cmeduski/40/4010.htm (accessed 18 Nov 2005).

22   www.idea.gov.uk/children/everychild1.pdf (accessed 16 Nov 2005).

23   Although schools face no official duty to cooperate, as other 'strategic bodies' do, the school inspection framework has been widened to include responsibility for children's well-being, in addition to traditional responsibilities concerning academic achievement.

24   M Power, *The Audit Explosion* (London: Demos, 1997).

25   C Argyris, *Flawed Advice and the Management Trap: How managers can know when they're getting good advice and when they're not* (Oxford: Oxford University Press, 1999).

26   Demos/CENTREX scenario planning course, 28 Sep 2005.

27   H Mintzberg, 'Crafting strategy', *Harvard Business Review* (Jul/Aug 1987).

28   As early as 1997 it was being argued that 'fragmentation of services for children has been held responsible for serious problems in meeting the needs of vulnerable children'; see Perri 6, *Holistic Government* (London: Demos, 1997).

29   D Chesterman and M Horne, *Local Authority?* (London: Demos, 2003).

30   *Victoria Climbié Inquiry.*

31   This is another area in which central government has adopted a useful practice, through establishing the five outcomes for children as the basis for the *Every Child Matters* reforms.

32   See, for instance, Hannah Lownsbrough's report on the development of Shotton Hall CAN Academy, available from www.can- online.org.uk/services/education.asp (accessed 16 Nov 2005).

33   M Gladwell, *The Tipping Point: How little things can make a big difference* (London, Abacus, 2002); also RM Kanter, BA Stein and TD Jick, *The Challenge of Organisational Change* (New York: Free Press, 1992).

34   P Senge, *The Fifth Discipline: The art and practice of the learning organisation* (New York: Doubleday and Century Business, 1990).

35   M Wheatley and M Kellner-Rogers, 'Bringing life to organisational change', *Journal for Strategic Performance Measurement* (April/ May1998).

36   Heifetz, *Leadership Without Easy Answers.*

37   DfES, *Every Child Matters: Next steps* (London: DfES, 2004).

38   V Iles and K Sutherland, *Organisational Change: A review for health care managers professionals and researchers* (London: National Co-ordinating Centre for Service Delivery and Organisation, 2001).

39   G Mulgan, 'Lessons of power', *Prospect* May 2005; see: www. prospectmagazine.co.uk/article_details.php?id=6888 (accessed 16 Nov 2005).

40   SH Alvord, DL Brown and CW Letts, *Social Entrepreneurship: Leadership that facilitates societal transformation – an exploratory study* (Cambridge, MA: Centre for Public Leadership, 2004).

41   Iles and Sutherland, *Organisational Change*; also, for an analysis of how a similar approach can be applied in national politics, see L Haynes and M Ignatieff, *Mobilizing Support for the United Nations* (Cambridge, MA: Centre for Public Leadership, 2004).

42   M Fullan, *Leading in a Culture of Change* (San Francisco, CA: Jossey-Bass, 2001).

43   *National Evaluation of Children's Trusts: Phase 1 interim report* (Norwich: UEA Norwich, 2004).

44   D Hargreaves, *Education Epidemic: How innovation networks can transform secondary schools* (London: Demos, 2003).

45   Power, *Risk Management of Everything*.

46   R Kelly, 'Reasons for raising the bar', speech to the Specialist Schools Trust, 4 Jul 2005.

47   See, for example, Tom Bentley's discussion of 'democratic management' in Bentley, *Everyday Democracy*.

48   www.bmjlearning.com/planrecord/assessment/cirIntro.jsp (accessed 16 Nov 2005).

49   C Handy, *Gods of Management: The changing work of organisations* (London: Arrow, 1995).

50   See: www.idea-knowledge.gov.uk/idk/core/page.do?pageId=73297 (accessed 21 Nov 2005).

51   Senge, *Fifth Discipline*.

52   G Binney and C Williams, *Leaning into the Future*, quoted in J MacBeath, 'Leadership: learning to live with contradiction'; see: www.ncsl.org.uk/media/ F7B/52/kpool-evidence-macbeath.pdf (accessed 17 Nov 2005).

53   M Bond et al, *Every Child Matters: Perspectives on community leadership* (Nottingham: National College for School Leadership, 2005).

54   Iles and Sutherland, *Organisational Change*.

55   DfES, *Every Child Matters: Change for children* (London: DfES, 2004); see: www.everychildmatters.gov.uk/publications/ (accessed 17 Nov 2005).

56   www.everychildmatters.gov.uk/aims/strategicoverview/ (accessed 16 Nov 2005).

57   D Goleman, *Emotional Intelligence: Why it can matter more than IQ* (London: Bloomsbury, 1996).

58   Ibid.

59   DfES, *Five Year Strategy for Children and Learners* (Norwich: TSO, 2004).

60   M Bichard, 'That's no way to act', *Public Finance*, 5 Aug 2005.

61   J Chapman, *System Failure: Why governments must learn to think differently* (London: Demos, 2002).

62   Annual performance assessment replaces the performance assessment of children's social care undertaken previously by the Social Services Inspectorate (SSI) and, latterly, by the Commission for Social Care Inspection (CSCI) and

the existing basis for the education rating used in the comprehensive performance assessment (CPA).

63   Joint area reviews will take place every three years. They will assess the quality of services and make judgements about how well all services in a local area (including those outside the statutory control of the local authority) work together to improve the well-being of children and young people.

64   Ofsted, *Framework for the Inspection of Schools in England from September 2005* (Norwich: TSO, 2004).

65   These can be found in DfES, *Every Child Matters: Change for children.*

66   *Guidance on the Children and Young People's Plan* (London: HM Government, 2005).

67   The guidance states, 'The CYPP does not need to be submitted to the DfES, but departmental advisers will wish to discuss the planning process, as well as progress in implementation, in their regular discussions with local partners.'

68   *Guidance on the Children and Young People's Plan.*

69   Ofsted, *Framework for the Inspection of Schools in England from September 2005.*

70   Select Committee Report, *Education and Skills – Ninth Report* (London: House of Commons, 2005).

71   Ofsted, *Every Child Matters: Arrangements for the annual performance assessment of council children's services* (London: Ofsted, 2005).

72   Quoted in Select Committee Report, *Education and Skills.*

73   DfES, *Five Year Strategy for Children and Learners.*

74   DfES, schools white paper, *Higher Standards, Better Schools for All.*

75   Ibid.

76   From NCSL/ContinYou conference, quoted in J Craig, *Taking the Wide View* (Nottingham: NCSL, forthcoming).

DEMOS – Licence to Publish

THE WORK (AS DEFINED BELOW) IS PROVIDED UNDER THE TERMS OF THIS LICENCE ("LICENCE"). THE WORK IS PROTECTED BY COPYRIGHT AND/OR OTHER APPLICABLE LAW. ANY USE OF THE WORK OTHER THAN AS AUTHORIZED UNDER THIS LICENCE IS PROHIBITED. BY EXERCISING ANY RIGHTS TO THE WORK PROVIDED HERE, YOU ACCEPT AND AGREE TO BE BOUND BY THE TERMS OF THIS LICENCE. DEMOS GRANTS YOU THE RIGHTS CONTAINED HERE IN CONSIDERATION OF YOUR ACCEPTANCE OF SUCH TERMS AND CONDITIONS.

1. Definitions

   a **"Collective Work"** means a work, such as a periodical issue, anthology or encyclopedia, in which the Work in its entirety in unmodified form, along with a number of other contributions, constituting separate and independent works in themselves, are assembled into a collective whole. A work that constitutes a Collective Work will not be considered a Derivative Work (as defined below) for the purposes of this Licence.

   b **"Derivative Work"** means a work based upon the Work or upon the Work and other pre-existing works, such as a musical arrangement, dramatization, fictionalization, motion picture version, sound recording, art reproduction, abridgment, condensation, or any other form in which the Work may be recast, transformed, or adapted, except that a work that constitutes a Collective Work or a translation from English into another language will not be considered a Derivative Work for the purpose of this Licence.

   c **"Licensor"** means the individual or entity that offers the Work under the terms of this Licence.

   d **"Original Author"** means the individual or entity who created the Work.

   e **"Work"** means the copyrightable work of authorship offered under the terms of this Licence.

   f **"You"** means an individual or entity exercising rights under this Licence who has not previously violated the terms of this Licence with respect to the Work, or who has received express permission from DEMOS to exercise rights under this Licence despite a previous violation.

2. Fair Use Rights. Nothing in this licence is intended to reduce, limit, or restrict any rights arising from fair use, first sale or other limitations on the exclusive rights of the copyright owner under copyright law or other applicable laws.

3. Licence Grant. Subject to the terms and conditions of this Licence, Licensor hereby grants You a worldwide, royalty-free, non-exclusive, perpetual (for the duration of the applicable copyright) licence to exercise the rights in the Work as stated below:

   a to reproduce the Work, to incorporate the Work into one or more Collective Works, and to reproduce the Work as incorporated in the Collective Works;

   b to distribute copies or phonorecords of, display publicly, perform publicly, and perform publicly by means of a digital audio transmission the Work including as incorporated in Collective Works;

The above rights may be exercised in all media and formats whether now known or hereafter devised. The above rights include the right to make such modifications as are technically necessary to exercise the rights in other media and formats. All rights not expressly granted by Licensor are hereby reserved.

4. Restrictions. The licence granted in Section 3 above is expressly made subject to and limited by the following restrictions:

   a You may distribute, publicly display, publicly perform, or publicly digitally perform the Work only under the terms of this Licence, and You must include a copy of, or the Uniform Resource Identifier for, this Licence with every copy or phonorecord of the Work You distribute, publicly display, publicly perform, or publicly digitally perform. You may not offer or impose any terms on the Work that alter or restrict the terms of this Licence or the recipients' exercise of the rights granted hereunder. You may not sublicence the Work. You must keep intact all notices that refer to this Licence and to the disclaimer of warranties. You may not distribute, publicly display, publicly perform, or publicly digitally perform the Work with any technological measures that control access or use of the Work in a manner inconsistent with the terms of this Licence Agreement. The above applies to the Work as incorporated in a Collective Work, but this does not require the Collective Work apart from the Work itself to be made subject to the terms of this Licence. If You create a Collective Work, upon notice from any Licencor You must, to the extent practicable, remove from the Collective Work any reference to such Licensor or the Original Author, as requested.

   b You may not exercise any of the rights granted to You in Section 3 above in any manner that is primarily intended for or directed toward commercial advantage or private monetary compensation. The exchange of the Work for other copyrighted works by means of digital file-sharing or otherwise shall not be considered to be intended for or directed toward commercial advantage or private monetary compensation, provided there is no payment of any monetary compensation in connection with the exchange of copyrighted works.

c If you distribute, publicly display, publicly perform, or publicly digitally perform the Work or any Collective Works, You must keep intact all copyright notices for the Work and give the Original Author credit reasonable to the medium or means You are utilizing by conveying the name (or pseudonym if applicable) of the Original Author if supplied; the title of the Work if supplied. Such credit may be implemented in any reasonable manner; provided, however, that in the case of a Collective Work, at a minimum such credit will appear where any other comparable authorship credit appears and in a manner at least as prominent as such other comparable authorship credit.

5. Representations, Warranties and Disclaimer
  a By offering the Work for public release under this Licence, Licensor represents and warrants that, to the best of Licensor's knowledge after reasonable inquiry:
    i Licensor has secured all rights in the Work necessary to grant the licence rights hereunder and to permit the lawful exercise of the rights granted hereunder without You having any obligation to pay any royalties, compulsory licence fees, residuals or any other payments;
    ii The Work does not infringe the copyright, trademark, publicity rights, common law rights or any other right of any third party or constitute defamation, invasion of privacy or other tortious injury to any third party.
  b EXCEPT AS EXPRESSLY STATED IN THIS LICENCE OR OTHERWISE AGREED IN WRITING OR REQUIRED BY APPLICABLE LAW, THE WORK IS LICENCED ON AN "AS IS" BASIS, WITHOUT WARRANTIES OF ANY KIND, EITHER EXPRESS OR IMPLIED INCLUDING, WITHOUT LIMITATION, ANY WARRANTIES REGARDING THE CONTENTS OR ACCURACY OF THE WORK.

6. Limitation on Liability. EXCEPT TO THE EXTENT REQUIRED BY APPLICABLE LAW, AND EXCEPT FOR DAMAGES ARISING FROM LIABILITY TO A THIRD PARTY RESULTING FROM BREACH OF THE WARRANTIES IN SECTION 5, IN NO EVENT WILL LICENSOR BE LIABLE TO YOU ON ANY LEGAL THEORY FOR ANY SPECIAL, INCIDENTAL, CONSEQUENTIAL, PUNITIVE OR EXEMPLARY DAMAGES ARISING OUT OF THIS LICENCE OR THE USE OF THE WORK, EVEN IF LICENSOR HAS BEEN ADVISED OF THE POSSIBILITY OF SUCH DAMAGES.

7. Termination
  a This Licence and the rights granted hereunder will terminate automatically upon any breach by You of the terms of this Licence. Individuals or entities who have received Collective Works from You under this Licence, however, will not have their licences terminated provided such individuals or entities remain in full compliance with those licences. Sections 1, 2, 5, 6, 7, and 8 will survive any termination of this Licence.
  b Subject to the above terms and conditions, the licence granted here is perpetual (for the duration of the applicable copyright in the Work). Notwithstanding the above, Licensor reserves the right to release the Work under different licence terms or to stop distributing the Work at any time; provided, however that any such election will not serve to withdraw this Licence (or any other licence that has been, or is required to be, granted under the terms of this Licence), and this Licence will continue in full force and effect unless terminated as stated above.

8. Miscellaneous
  a Each time You distribute or publicly digitally perform the Work or a Collective Work, DEMOS offers to the recipient a licence to the Work on the same terms and conditions as the licence granted to You under this Licence.
  b If any provision of this Licence is invalid or unenforceable under applicable law, it shall not affect the validity or enforceability of the remainder of the terms of this Licence, and without further action by the parties to this agreement, such provision shall be reformed to the minimum extent necessary to make such provision valid and enforceable.
  c No term or provision of this Licence shall be deemed waived and no breach consented to unless such waiver or consent shall be in writing and signed by the party to be charged with such waiver or consent.
  d This Licence constitutes the entire agreement between the parties with respect to the Work licensed here. There are no understandings, agreements or representations with respect to the Work not specified here. Licensor shall not be bound by any additional provisions that may appear in any communication from You. This Licence may not be modified without the mutual written agreement of DEMOS and You.